Praise for *The Person Called You*

Bill Hendricks was instrumental for me in discovering and clarifying my calling during the first quarter of my career. Discovering our purpose in life is one of the most important questions we can ask. Bill helps you practically answer that question with *The Person Called You*. I highly recommend this book!

BRAD LOMENICK, author, *The Catalyst Leader*

Bill's perspective and stories from his own walk with Jesus bring many fresh insights to a problem we all face: how do we know what God is calling us to do?

MATT CARTER, pastor of preaching and vision at Austin Stone Community Church, Texas; coauthor, *The Real Win*

Bill Hendricks has spent a lifetime helping people answer three questions: Who am I *now*? Where do I fit *now*? and What do I contribute *in the next season of my life*? He has developed the tools and wisdom required. He is the master of his craft, ushering you into the next season of life's journey.

BOB BUFORD, author, *Halftime* and *Drucker & Me*

Finally, somebody who gets it—it IS all about you! You are the only YOU we've got. And if you don't become YOU we're going to miss YOU! In this insightful volume, Bill uses his own giftedness to help you discover yours.

REGGIE MCNEAL, author, *A Work of Heart*; missional leadership specialist for Leadership Network

The Person Called You is the culmination of Bill's best thinking. Reading and applying the message of this book will give you insight into what God had in mind when He created you.

RANDY FRAZEE, senior minister, Oak Hills Church, San Antonio, Texas, and author, *Making Room for Life*

Want to explore what makes you unique and what can drive you in life? What causes giftedness to thrive or fail? How should you think about your gifts and fit at work? How you fit with others in your life? This book will help you discover what can make you an even better YOU for the Father who created you and made you the way you are.

DR. DARRELL BOCK, executive director of cultural engagement, The Hendricks Center; professor of New Testament Studies, Dallas Theological Seminary

A valuable, easy-to-understand guide for discovering what in the world you were made for. Bill Hendricks' insight into giftedness has helped me navigate my own life's direction.

PEGGY WEHMEYER, former correspondent, ABC News

Bill Hendricks is speaking to anyone who slows down to ponder the power found in *The Person Called You*. He is among the few who both know God intimately and have the ability to help others know themselves.

BOB SHANK, founder/CEO, The Master's Program

Written in a personal and warm style and filled with numerous practical lessons from history, the Bible, and years of experience with clients, Bill Hendricks has written a balanced and thoughtful book on how to discover our unique giftedness and put it to work in meaningful and fulfilling service to God and others.

DR. GARY COOK, president, Dallas Baptist University

Many people have no meaningful vision for their work. What sort of work should they be doing? What is work all about? Bill Hendricks offers some profound insights into these core questions through this timely book. He's done a real service in showing us how intimately God is involved in who we are and the work we do.

ANDY MILLS, entrepreneur and former CEO, Thompson Financial and Professional Publishing Group

This book is a confidence-builder, not in a hyped-up way, but with solid, practical grounding in a way that will last and grow long after you finish the book. Read *The Person Called You* to become more comfortable in your own skin, and more understanding of others.

DR. BRAD SMITH, president, Bakke Graduate University

Defining your own giftedness is many times difficult. Bill Hendricks' step-by-step guide to discovering your giftedness will help you in any area of life to determine how to find your distinctive gifts and purpose, and then how to leverage them to become the best you can be. If you're looking for clarity and purpose, this is the book to read.

TODD RHOADES, Monday Morning Insight; director of New Media and Technology Initiatives, Leadership Network

In an eminently readable and provocative work, Bill Hendricks strikes a death blow to the blasé rumors of "I'm just like everybody else" and "Do I really have anything special to offer to myself and others with my life?" Read the pages and learn!

DR. DAVID FLETCHER, founder and host, XPastor

The Person Called You is a deeply insightful, conversational, and welcoming guide to discovering one's giftedness, identity, and vocation. A wonderful help for those struggling with their own sense of calling and purpose.

CHERIE HARDER, president, The Trinity Forum

We all want joy and meaning in our life, but too often we stumble around and settle for much less. This book provides a thoughtful, clear process for determining how God made each of us, and how we can best realize God's plan for our life.

KERRY KNOTT, president, C.S. Lewis Institute

Is there a way to take what you enjoy doing and what you are motivated to do and turn this into a career? Bill's book offers insight into how we might take personal inventory and then match the results to potential career opportunities. A practical, insightful book for recent graduates, mid-career people, and even those contemplating retirement.

DR. AL ERISMAN, executive in residence and former director for the Center for Integrity in Business, Seattle Pacific University; editor, *Ethix Magazine*

Focusing on our unique giftedness and our stories of flourishing, Hendricks helps us discover who we are and what God has made us to do. I'm going to have this book on hand when people seek my counsel about what they should do with their lives. I'm grateful to Bill Hendricks for sharing his wisdom in such a readable and compelling way.

DR. MARK D. ROBERTS, executive director of digital media, the High Calling, H. E. Butt Foundation

The giftedness assessment that Bill offers will assist individuals in understanding how to use their gifts to enhance quality of life for themselves, as well as for others they will influence throughout their lives. It is my hope that women and men will read this book and be compelled to use their gifts to make a difference in their work and their relationships.

DR. BECKY PANEITZ, president and CEO, Inseitz Group; former president, Northwest Arkansas Community College

Bill Hendricks knows what makes people tick. My family and I have been through his process, as have key executives at my company. This book grows out of decades of real-world experience with everyday people facing some of the most important decisions in their lives. Bill's message about giftedness proved to be a godsend for me. I know it will be for you, as well.

ROBERT M. BRIGGS, president and CEO, Briggs Freeman Sotheby's International Realty

This book contains the author's lessons of a lifetime on the important subject of giftedness. It is written with a typical Hendricks flair—it holds your attention, even in our digital age, when attention spans are short. This is one fine book!

DR. DAVID NAUGLE, professor, Dallas Baptist University; author, *Philosophy: A Student's Guide*

Bill explains simply how we can see a clear path to who we are, not what we do. He helps us see our unique wiring, to see ourselves through commonsense lenses. When you see yourself clearly, you'll be surprised how clearly you'll see. And once in focus, you'll see how you can be the person you are meant to be.

DR. MICHAEL EASLEY, teaching pastor, Fellowship Bible Church, Brentwood, Tennessee; cohost, *InContext*; former president, Moody Bible Institute

In *The Person Called You*, Bill has provided us with a well-researched, biblically grounded, scholarly, yet accessible tool that moves beyond mere diagnostic tests to a genuine theology of vocation. I not only commend this fine volume to the church with great joy, but do so with a prayer that many will read it and apply the wisdom that Bill teaches.

DR. TONY JEFFREY, headmaster, Providence Christian School of Texas

This book is the perfect resource for teachers, counselors, youth workers, and anyone else trying to help others find their path in life. I strongly urge you to buy two copies of this book—one for yourself and the other for someone who is looking to you for guidance and direction.

MICHAEL MILTON, PHD, teaching pastor, Truth in Action Ministries

We see it all the time. Because of ego or cultural or corporate expectations, people try to be something they aren't, and the results are less than attractive and productive. Bill has hit the nail on the head. When people appreciate their individuality, embrace their giftedness, and humbly leverage it, their level of job satisfaction and service to those around them skyrockets.

DR. TOMMY THOMAS, lead partner, Job*Fit*Matters, Nashville, Tennessee

THE PERSON CALLED
YOU

WHY YOU'RE HERE,
WHY YOU MATTER &
WHAT YOU SHOULD
DO WITH YOUR LIFE

BILL HENDRICKS

MOODY PUBLISHERS

CHICAGO

All Scripture quotations, unless otherwise indicated, are taken from the *New American Standard Bible*®,
Copyright © 1960, 1962, 1963, 1968, 1971, 1972, 1973, 1975, 1977, 1995 by The Lockman Foundation. Used
by permission. (www.Lockman.org)
Scripture quotations marked NIV are taken from the Holy Bible, New International Version®, NIV®.
Copyright © 1973, 1978, 1984, 2011 by Biblica, Inc.™
Used by permission of Zondervan. All rights reserved worldwide. www.zondervan.com. The "NIV" and
"New International Version" are trademarks registered in the United States Patent and Trademark Office by
Biblica, Inc.™
Scripture quotations marked THE MESSAGE are from *The Message*, copyright © by Eugene H. Peterson
1993, 1994, 1995. Used by permission of NavPress Publishing Group.

Edited by Elizabeth Cody Newenhuyse
Cover design: Dean Renninger
Interior design: Smartt Guys design
Cover image: Thumbprint: Stock.XCHNG #227873

All websites and phone numbers listed herein are accurate at the time of publication but may change in the
future or cease to exist. The listing of website references and resources does not imply publisher endorsement
of the site's entire contents. Groups and organizations are listed for informational purposes, and listing does
not imply publisher endorsement of their activities

Library of Congress Cataloging-in-Publication Data

Hendricks, Bill.
 The person called you : why you're here, why you matter & what you should do with your life /
Bill Hendricks.
   pages cm
 Summary: ""I can't stand my job anymore." "I feel like I have no direction." "What should I really be doing
with my life?" "What's my purpose?"Sound familiar? For the past twenty years, Bill Hendricks has been
helping people of all ages and stages stymied by those kinds of questions. The key is found in harnessing the
power of their giftedness. Every person has their own unique giftedness. Including you. And the best way to
discover it is not through a test or an inventory or a gift assessment exercise, but from your own life story.The
Person Called You is a celebration, exploration, and explanation of human giftedness. Bill describes what
it is (and isn't), where it comes from, how you can discover your own giftedness, and most importantly, its
potential to transform your life. Especially your work and relationships. Rather than just paying lip service
to the popular notion that "everyone is unique," Bill puts a fine point on just how unique you really are, and
how your personhood and purpose are inseparably linked.You're not just a "type" of person. You're you!
With a unique way of doing life that fits you for a particular calling. Honor that God-given wiring and you'll
start waking up with a sense of meaning, purpose, confidence, and direction. No, your problems won't all be
solved. The world doesn't work that way. But as Bill shows through the stories of people he's worked with, it
works a lot better when people use their giftedness to make their best contribution.The Person Called You
is a practical guide to living the life you were meant to live. It's for anyone who knows they aren't quite where
they ought to be-where they would flourish-and wants to start being who they were made to be. Is that really
possible? Absolutely. It all begins with what Bill calls the "good truth" about you. "-- Provided by publisher.
 Includes bibliographical references.
 ISBN 978-0-8024-1201-0 (paperback)
 1. Ability. 2. Conduct of life. I. Title.
 BF431.H389 2014
 158.1--dc23

                                                        2014013762

We hope you enjoy this book from Moody Publishers. Our goal is to provide
high-quality, thought-provoking books and products that connect truth to your real needs and challenges.
For more information on other books and products written and produced from a biblical perspective, go to
www.moodypublishers.com or write to:

Moody Publishers
820 N. LaSalle Boulevard
Chicago, IL 60610

3 5 7 9 10 8 6 4 2

Printed in the United States of America

This book is dedicated to my clients. I've learned the most from them. Many of them I remember, not by name but by their stories. Some have become good friends and even close friends. Thank you all for writing this book. I'm just the wordsmith.

CONTENTS

THE QUESTION

Somewhere in my twenties I discovered Sherlock Holmes. Which is to say, I devoured Sherlock Holmes. I bought all of the stories and read them through like a man possessed. I was captivated by Holmes's magical powers of observation, ruthlessly analytical mind, and boxer-like ability to drive a point home.

I especially loved the way Holmes would come alive whenever a new client showed up at 33B Baker Street and presented their situation. As they unfolded their tale, his eyes would light up and he'd cry, "You fill me with interest!" That was the signal that the game was on and the master was engaged.

In truth, I was taken with Sherlock Holmes because I imagined myself having people come to me with their mysteries and riddles and ask me to put my brain on their case. There was something highly appealing about being able to look at a set of factors that seem totally mystifying to someone else, offer them a solution, have them exclaim, "That's amazing! How did you do that?" only to reply, "Elementary, my dear Watson."

"WHICH WAY DO I GO?"

Thirty years later I'm a lot less interested in impressing people than in impacting them in some positive way. For it turns out that, like Sherlock Holmes, I too have a boutique consulting practice where people come seeking answers to important questions in their life.

They come for a variety of reasons. Many feel lost or lacking in direction: "I've arrived at this point in my life, and I just don't know what to do or which way to go. I'm lost!" Somehow the highway of life is no longer providing signs or markers, and they feel like they're just making things up as they go along. They're not sure where they're headed, so how in the world can they possibly know how to get there? They come seeking direction.

Others feel a lack of confidence. They don't know what they don't know, and they know that. They feel uncertain, hesitant. Maybe they have a notion about going to grad school or taking a particular job, but they don't want to make a mistake. Or maybe they have an inkling about what they ought to do with their life, or even a dream they've nursed since childhood, but they're afraid to pull the trigger on it. What if they're wrong? It's as if they need permission to succeed. Certainly they are seeking reassurance, affirmation, and a sense of confidence to move forward.

> "I used to dream about that 'perfect' job. But that was unrealistic. In the end you just get a job. Now I know why they call it work."

Often I'll see the bored individual who's been plodding along in life, doing what they're supposed to do. But they have a vague sense that there must be something more. They see other people living with zest and energy and passion, employed in cool jobs and achieving great things. They're kind of puzzled: Why hasn't that happened for me? Is it even possible for me? Or am I just fated to live an average, ho-hum existence? They'd love to find some inspiration and a new lease on life, or at least a change for the better.

Closely related to the bored person is the person who feels stuck. A lot of men in midlife call me with that complaint: "Bill, I've been doing this career for twenty-five years, and I really don't want to retire doing it. I'd love to do something else, but I don't know what that would be. I don't know what my other options are." Clearly they're looking for a new path.

Some people come out of outright frustration. They've been trying and trying, but for whatever reason, their life just doesn't seem to be working. Maybe they've gone through a string of jobs and can't find anything that works. Their spouse is getting tired of it all and keeps asking why they can't "get their act together." They're kind of wondering the same thing. Some admit that they hate their life. Is there anything I can tell them that would turn things around?

Discouragement also drives a lot of people my way. Life has not turned out the way they had hoped. At one time they had a dream of getting paid to do exciting and meaningful work. But that hasn't happened. Instead they took that entry-level job out of college, went to work at a company, got married, took out a mortgage and a car payment, had a couple of kids, and settled into a routine. Now life seems all about keeping the boss satisfied and paying the bills. As one man in his early thirties put it, "I've given up. I used to dream about that 'perfect' job. But that was unrealistic. In the end you just get a job. Now I know why they call it work." A person like that is desperately looking for some hope.

And then there are people who are totally burned out. Some of them have been remarkably successful and extremely well paid. But they're tired. They're weary. They've had enough. It doesn't matter if their employer offers them more money. They're looking for a way out. As much as anything, they're looking for rest—not just a vacation but something deeper, something freeing and fresh in their heart and soul.

In the past decade a torrent of Millennials have come my way, young adults in their twenties. Our culture does not know how to get someone from high school graduation into the adult world of work. As a result, countless Millennials are totally at sea trying to figure out which way to go. Many of them have college degrees and are very bright. But they haven't found a job, at least not one that can support them. Their self-esteem is eroding by the day, and as they look ahead to the world their Boomer parents are leaving them, they feel increasingly cynical. Others have parlayed their degree into a first job, only to find that it wasn't the career they thought it would be. Now what?

Slightly older than the Millennials are the people who have gotten a professional degree and, several years into the field, wake up one day and realize they've made a terrible mistake. Law, or accounting, or medicine, or whatever was not for them! Often they've got significant school loans to pay off, so they feel trapped. They know they can't stay where they are, but they can't afford to just walk away from it. What should they do?

Of course, not everyone who comes my way has a problem. Some people come to talk about their future because they want to be intentional about embracing that future. This is especially the case for people in midlife who want to have what a friend calls a "constructive midlife crisis." Why have an affair or buy a toy when it's so much more interesting to engage your energies in a meaningful pursuit?

Nor are all who seek significance aging Boomers. A lot of young adults don't want to wait to live a life that matters. They want to start down that path from the get-go.

WHEN I FELT STUPID

I could go on and on about the different reasons people look me up. I always feel compassion when I hear their stories, because my story is very similar.

I was thirty years old when it was time to answer The Question. It's the question everyone faces in their twenties: *What should I do with my life?*

My wife at the time, Nancy, was tired of putting me through graduate schools. She was ready to start having babies, so now it was my turn to go out and earn a living.

Everyone assumed I would have no problem doing that. I kept hearing things like, "Bill, you're so bright. You graduated from Harvard. You've got two master's degrees. Why, you can do anything you want!"

Maybe. Except for one small problem: I had no clue what I wanted to do.

Let me tell you, it doesn't matter how intelligent you may be or what academic degrees you may have: if you don't know what to do with your life, you feel really stupid. And I felt very, very stupid.

I felt like I wanted to do something "important" with my life. So that was a start. But what did that mean? I had no idea. Perhaps because my father was a seminary professor and I had grown up in a culture where faith mattered a lot, I had some vague notion that I should go into "the ministry." But I didn't want to be a pastor (at the time, my opinion of pastors was low). Neither did I want to be a missionary (at the time, my opinion of missionaries was even lower). And I sure didn't want to be a seminary professor (I mean, why just copy my dad, right?).

I had other wild ideas floating around in my head. Maybe I ought to go into the corporate world. I looked over a brochure for Harvard Business School, and their case method approach totally appealed to me. But wait—that was yet another graduate degree. No way would Nancy stand for that!

> All the faith in the world can't replace the discomfort of walking around in life not knowing why you're here.

I also had this whole creative thing going. I had flirted with the idea of becoming a professional musician. But that hardly seemed like a way to support a family. I loved film and photography. But I'd gone to Harvard to study English, not to USC to study film, so I was hopelessly behind the curve in that competitive field.

I had (and have) a vivid imagination, so I had thought of a thousand other interesting possibilities for what to do for a career. But the moment of truth was at hand. Nancy had "called the question," as they say. It was time to come up with an answer: *What should I do with my life?*

PITFALLS, BREAKDOWNS, DETOURS, AND BLIND ALLEYS

Looking back, I could easily have ended up like any number of the people I've described above: lost, uncertain, frustrated, discouraged, bored, trapped, burned out, depressed, cynical. I'm a person of faith, and many of my clients have been people with far more faith than I'll ever have. But all the faith in the world can't replace the discomfort of walking around in life not knowing why you're here.

How do people end up in such a fix? I've discovered that a thousand roads lead there. Some get there by thinking there's some sort of script you're supposed to follow. Play by the rules and you'll go to the top. Many parents are especially guilty of writing such a script for their children, outlining certain activities, certain friends, certain schools, certain majors, certain fraternities or sororities, and certain careers that supposedly will guarantee success. I've met countless people who followed such a script. Sure enough, they're successful. But they hate their life nonetheless.

On the other hand, a lot of people have just lived randomly. They've come at life with absolutely no purpose or direction. Like the lady who was doing research for a mining company. How did she end up in that field? "I wanted to go to the University of Texas and major in broadcasting, but my boyfriend was going to Penn State, so I applied there instead. I had to have a scholarship, and they only had one left. It was in mineral sciences, so that's what I majored in." Seriously?

A similar case was the lawyer who came to see me because he was tired of working at his firm. I asked him how he got into law in the first place. "In college I was in a fraternity. One day some fraternity brothers were talking about going to law school. I thought, 'That sounds cool.' So I took the LSAT and applied where one of them applied, and I got accepted." That's how much thought that guy put into choosing a career!

> Frankly, sometimes I'm amazed that anybody ends up in work that fits them!

Some people have a plan, and it's a good plan, and everything is fine, even the money part. Then life intervenes. They get laid off or fired. They get served with divorce papers, or maybe their spouse dies. They get sick or disabled. Their kids leave home or they take early retirement, and suddenly they've got time on their hands. Or maybe they sell a business, or gain an inheritance, or (God forbid) hit the lottery, and now they've got a whole new set of problems trying to manage some money. Any major life change can upset the apple cart, and a plan that looked so good is suddenly out the window.

Lots of people end up where they end up because their internal GPS gets programmed early on with bad data. For instance, their parents told them things that were well-intentioned, but totally bogus. Like, "Son, whatever you do, don't go into business for yourself. Your grandfather did that and it cost him everything he owned." Or, "Honey, there's two kinds of people in this world: the people who control the money and the people who don't. You need to be one of the people who controls the money, or else marry someone who does." Or, "Here's a report that says there will be a shortage of chemical engineers in ten years. Why don't you major in chemical engineering?" Or, "You'll never make a living as an actor. You took a test that said you're good with numbers. You should go into accounting. As long as this country has a tax code, you'll never want for a job."

Perhaps the granddaddy of all crocks is the very popular canard, "You can become anything you want to be." Really? I grant that in the United States and other free societies, people have options. So in that sense they can choose whatever career path they desire. But no one gets to choose their personhood and essential identity. Shape it? Yes. Cultivate it? Yes. Give it education and experience? Yes. But as we'll see, you are born who you are, and no amount of wishing, praying, educating, training, mentoring, incentivizing, coercing, or forcing can ever change who you fundamentally are.

I could fill a book with all the bad advice that parents, teachers, coaches, and other adults give to young people. Frankly, sometimes I'm amazed that anybody ends up in work that fits them!

And then there's the huge undertow of outright lies, abuse, wounds, and curses that will ultimately drag someone underwater. How can a young man ever feel completely confident and competent when he grows up hearing his father tell him over and over, "You're no good. You'll never amount to anything"? Or consider the impact on a teenage girl whose parent tells her, "I cried when you were born because I was hoping you'd be a boy." And then there's the woman who tells her ex, whose gifts incline toward the creative arts, "No woman will ever marry you again, because you can't support a wife!" If comments like these wound your spirit before you even begin the race, it will be almost impossible to run it very well.

THE DISCOVERY

And so I do feel great compassion for the people who come my way, because they are almost always good people who haven't done anything wrong. But a lot of them think they must have done something wrong, or that there's something wrong with them. So they're surprised when I tell them, no, actually, what they're experiencing is quite common and rather normal (sad to say).

That's small consolation, I realize, but it's important to say nonetheless. If you're experiencing anything along the lines of what I'm describing here, you need to know that you're not alone, even though you may feel very alone.

In fact, you may be in the same boat as Socrates, a Greek philosopher who lived around 500 BCE. It was said of Socrates that he had a voice in his head that always told him what *not* to do but never what *to* do. A lot of people nowadays have that same voice in their head.

I certainly did when I was thirty and trying to answer The Question. I clearly knew what I didn't want to do (or so I thought at the time), but as I've said, I had no clue what I did want to do.

My saving grace was a book that an assistant dean encouraged me to obtain as I was finishing up my graduate degree in mass communications. That book was my first formal encounter with the phenomenon of human giftedness.

A few years later I was introduced to some folks who had taken the study of giftedness to a very high level, and they helped me discover my own giftedness. All I can say is: it changed my life. I don't mean it simply encouraged me or gave me a little bit of guidance or direction. I mean it transformed the way I see life and do life. "Transformed" is a bold word, I know. But that's what happened.

For the last twenty years, I've been helping people discover their giftedness. The vast majority have gained so much insight and direction from waking up to that reality that it has transformed the course of their lives, as it did mine.

You see, everyone—especially anyone who is a knowledge worker—is more or less compelled to come up with his or her answer to The Question: *What should I do with my life?*

I don't pretend to have the final word on the subject. But I do believe I've been blessed to have stumbled upon an invaluable clue that speaks to the heart of the matter.

THIS BOOK IS ABOUT *YOU*

But now, let me offer a word of caution from the outset. We live in a "fast" society, where people have come to expect instant solutions requiring minimal effort. I can relate to that. I'm as busy (and impatient) as the next person. I don't care for people giving me more information than I want to know. I just want them to cut to the chase.

But when we get to the question of what you should do with your life, we jump from everyday concerns to a whole different level of importance. Now we're playing for keeps! And so my appeal to anyone who wants to settle these matters with a brief, breezy treatment offering a quick fix is: slow down! Relax! Take a deep breath. What's the rush? You've got your whole life to live. You don't want it to be a superficial life of no consequence, do you? I doubt you'd have picked up this book if you did. But that's exactly what happens to people who settle for easy, superficial answers.

So let this book be about you. Just sip and savor it. No need to read it through in one sitting (unless you happen to be snowed in at a secluded cabin for a long weekend—not a bad idea!). Use it as you need to. Pull it off the shelf occasionally whenever you feel doubt about whether you matter and where you're headed. Think of it as an ongoing conversation between you and me as you navigate your particular path toward trying to live a meaningful life. (Of course, if you'd prefer to talk with me about all this in person, I can arrange for that. But a book seems like the most efficient and cost-effective way for both of us to begin the conversation.)

AN "OWNER'S MANUAL"

So exactly how would I work with you if you were to come to my own version of 33B Baker Street? Where would I begin? Well, first I'd listen to you and make sure I was clear on what your version of The Question is. You don't wake up in the morning and say, "I don't think I'm going to make it through today if I don't find out what my giftedness is." No! You wake up with a very practical, personal Question, along the lines of what I described earlier. I first need to know what that Question is.

But once I find out, I then show you something, something akin to an owner's manual on you. If you were planning to work on a car or a computer or some other sophisticated piece of equipment, you'd check the owner's manual first to find out: What was this machine designed to do? What does it do best? What does it take to get it to do that? What other pieces of equipment does it need around it to function most effectively? And maybe the most important information of all: What are the warning labels for this equipment for what *not* to do with it or to it?

Wouldn't it be wonderful if you had come into the world with an owner's manual like that? Well, in fact you have. There actually is a sort of "owner's manual" that can be developed for you. It is discoverable through a remarkable phenomenon, one shared by all human beings, which we call your giftedness.

IT ALL DEPENDS ON
YOUR GIFTEDNESS

1

A PATTERN IN YOUR LIFE

Certain things just are. We call such a thing a phenomenon. Take gravity, for example. Gravity is a phenomenon. You don't have to know anything about gravity to take advantage of it. It's just the way the world is.

Well, there's a phenomenon that shapes all human beings (including you). Here's how it works. Every person really is unique. As in one-of-a-kind. That uniqueness manifests itself through the person's behavior. It turns out that every individual lives out a pattern of behavior again and again throughout their life. It's the most natural way for them to function. Indeed, they don't think of doing life any other way.

HOW WARREN BUFFETT BECAME RICH

Later I'll show you how to detect your own pattern. For now, let me just pick someone who is well known and about whom we have lots of data from which to draw some conclusions: Warren Buffett, the world-renowned investor.

In 2003, a Wall Street analyst named Alice Schroeder took a leave of absence from Morgan Stanley to engage in a biographical study of

Warren Buffett's life. With his full cooperation, the project culminated in *The Snowball: Warren Buffett and the Business of Life.* The book is fascinating from many angles, but I regard it as a textbook case in demonstrating the phenomenon of giftedness.

Schroeder tells us that from childhood, Buffett displayed a fascination bordering on an obsession with numbers and the analysis of numbers. For example, as a boy in church: "He liked the sermons, he was bored by the rest of the service; he passed the time by calculating the life span of hymn composers from their birth and death dates in the hymnals. . . . He assumed that hymn composers would live longer than average. Living longer than average seemed to him an important goal."[1]

Sometimes he would sit on his friend's porch in Omaha, Nebraska, writing down the license-plate numbers of passing cars. He liked calculating the frequency of the letters and numbers used on the plates.

At six he began selling gum in his neighborhood—never single sticks, only packs of five—for a nickel. Soon he was buying six-packs of Coca Cola for 25 cents, then reselling single bottles for 5 cents, a 20 percent profit. Young Warren's favorite toy was—what else?—a money changer.

> Buffett confidently told his family he would be a millionaire by the time he was thirty-five.

The tradition in Buffett's family was for each child, when they were ten, to accompany their father to the East Coast to visit the sites they most wanted to see. For Warren the choice was easy: New York City, to visit the Scott Stamp and Coin Company, the Lionel Train Company (Warren spent hours poring over Lionel catalogues), and the New York Stock Exchange.

Not long after that, Buffett came across a library book entitled *One Thousand Ways to Make $1,000* (in the 1940s, $1,000 was a lot of money). He devoured the book, especially the concept of compounding. He became fascinated by the way that "numbers exploded as they grew at a constant rate over time," such that even "a small sum could eventually grow into a fortune. He could picture the numbers compounding as vividly as the way a snowball grew when he rolled it across the lawn" (hence the title of the book). "Warren began to think about time in a different way. Compounding married the present to the future. If a dollar today was going to be worth ten some years from now, then in his mind the two were the same."[2]

With that insight, Buffett confidently told his family he would be a millionaire by the time he was thirty-five.

In college Buffett read *The Intelligent Investor*, by Benjamin Graham. According to his roommate, "It was almost like he found a god." Ben Graham was teaching at Columbia University in New York, along with his colleague David Dodd. Together they had coauthored a seminal text entitled *Security Analysis*. Buffett determined he would go to graduate school there and study under these wizards of finance and investing.

Upon graduating, he wanted more than anything else to work for Graham's investment firm, Graham-Newman. But Graham turned him down. That did not deter Buffett. He returned to Omaha and became a stockbroker, but he continued to correspond with his mentor. He sent him stock tips and occasionally visited New York to see him. Finally, in 1954, Graham and his partner hired Buffett.

For two years, he worked as a securities analyst, quickly making himself the darling of the firm. Then Ben Graham announced he was retiring. Buffett was invited to become a general partner, but he declined. Without Graham, he had no interest in working at a New York investment firm.

So Buffett again returned to Omaha. At twenty-six, he had already made enough money to retire (when he began his studies at Colombia, Buffet had $9,800 in assets; since then his shrewd investments had grown 61 percent annually to $174,000). But he was eager to reach his goal of becoming a millionaire. So he formed a partnership named Buffett Associates, Ltd., and invited just six family members and close friends to join him. They all put in $105,000. Buffett put in $100.

The rest, as they say, is history. Buffett's company (later renamed Berkshire-Hathaway) is now the ninth leading public company in the world, worth an estimated $250 billion. The firm's annual growth in book value has averaged 19.7 percent to shareholders for the last forty-eight years (compared to 9.4 percent from companies listed on Standard & Poor's). Buffett himself is believed to hold $62 billion of personal wealth.

EVERYONE HAS A PATTERN

You can see a consistent pattern throughout Warren Buffett's life, from childhood to the present. He keeps using certain abilities, like analyzing, assessing worth, and recognizing patterns and anomalies. He keeps working with certain subject matter, like numbers, the concept of compounding, and business information. He prefers to do things on his own, and in his own way. When he wants to learn about something, he likes to go directly to the source, to the person who knows the most about it. And of course he measures his results by the dispassionate metric of profit. Many other aspects of Buffett's pattern could be cited from Schroeder's book.

Here's what's important: *every person has their own unique pattern of behavior and motivation.* That pattern begins in childhood and remains consistent throughout their life. Others may have similar patterns, but no two people have exactly the same pattern.

I could illustrate this phenomenon of a motivational pattern with countless other well-known people: Bill Gates, Steve Jobs, Oprah Winfrey, Winston Churchill, Adolf Hitler, Michelangelo, Mother Teresa, Martin Luther King Jr., Leonard Bernstein, Karl Wallenda, Lyndon Johnson, Jim Henson, Judy Garland, C. S. Lewis, Peter Drucker, Evel Knievel, Wolfgang Amadeus Mozart, Ben Carson, Margaret Thatcher, Nelson Mandela, I. M. Pei, Alexander the Great, John James Audubon. The list is endless.

"But Bill," I hear someone saying, "those are all world-class people. That wouldn't be the case for everyday folks."

Actually, it is—for two reasons. First, because *everyone*—including all of the people I mentioned—starts out as "everyday folks." No one is born world-class. But when a so-called average person follows their pattern, they may well end up at the world-class level.

But now let's define what we mean by "world class." That's not the same as having celebrity status. Someone can be world-famous, but not world-class. World-class means being among the best in the world at what you do. Whether or not anyone else knows about it is another story.

By that measure, I could tell you about teachers, appliance repair guys, mechanics, storytellers, editors, waiters, toll booth collectors, missionaries, bank tellers, and countless other no-name people who function at a world-class level.

Fame is just a distraction. Our aim in life ought not to become famous but to become the best at what we do.

Not only are all of us born as "everyday folks," we all have a pattern. Everyone! You. Me. The members of our families. Our friends. Our neighbors. Our coworkers. Our allies. Our enemies. Everyone.

How can I be so sure about that? Because for the last fifty years and more, a handful of people (myself among them) have engaged in a methodical, objective process of discovering people's patterns in order to help them make strategic decisions, both personally and professionally. Hundreds of thousands of individuals have gone through that process. Every single one of them had a pattern. No one has ever been found who doesn't have a pattern. When you find that kind of consistency, you conclude that human beings by their nature function according to patterns. In other words, there's a phenomenon at work. It's just the way the world is.

GIFTEDNESS—AND YOU

Does that phenomenon have a name? Actually it has many names. For example, we say that someone has a certain "bent" or "style." Or that someone is "wired" to do a certain thing. Or that someone is operating in their "sweet spot." The French have a wonderful word for it, "métier," meaning an area of activity in which one excels. And of course, we've all heard someone explain a person's behavior by saying, "Oh, he's just being Fred," or, "That is *so* like Sherry," and somehow we know exactly what they mean. We instinctively recognize people's patterns, even if we know nothing about the phenomenon.

> Giftedness is not just what you can do but what you are born to do, enjoy doing, and do well.

The term I use for the way that people live out their patterns is *giftedness*. It's not the most elegant term, but I haven't yet found a better one. It's also a term I hear a lot of people using nowadays, but I don't think most of them really know what they're talking about.

So let me offer a definition:

Giftedness is the unique way in which you function. It's a set of inborn core strengths and natural motivation you instinctively and consistently use to do things that you find satisfying and productive. Giftedness is not just what you can do but what you are born to do, enjoy doing, and do well.

Notice the words "inborn," "natural," and "instinctively." They point to the fact that giftedness is just that—a gift. Your giftedness is not something you acquire or go to school to get. It's just there, in you. You didn't ask for it. You didn't have to pay for it. It's just you.

Let me be clear about how I'm using the term *giftedness*. In popular culture, we call people "gifted" if they show unusual talent—superstars like Michael Jordan, James Taylor, Meryl Streep, Stephen Hawking, Michael Phelps. I won't argue that such people are amazing. And there is undoubtedly a correlation between their giftedness and the thing they do.

> If everyone has giftedness, then why do so many people hate their jobs?

But giftedness is, in fact, common. Not all of us rise to "world-class" status (although I suspect we have more Michael Jordans and Oprah Winfreys walking around than we realize). As we've already seen, each of us displays a consistent pattern of behavior, which is expressed even in the everyday, mundane affairs of life. What we wear, who we associate with, what kind of car we drive, who we vote for, what our religious convictions are (if any), what we watch on TV or click on online—all are part of our unique pattern.

Giftedness is not for a fortunate few. It is part of the human condition.

Perhaps one reason why "gifted" is so often applied to the elite is because certain children in schools are determined to be exceptional learners and given enhanced learning opportunities, called "talented and gifted" (TAG) programs or "gifted and talented education" (GATE or G/T). I'm all for these endeavors. But I still hold that all children, regardless of IQ or any other scale of functioning, possess their own form of giftedness—their own particular pattern of motivated behavior.

Is giftedness related to intelligence? No. Even someone who functions at a low level will display a bent toward a particular way of "doing life."

Is giftedness related to your work? We'll be looking at this later, but no, giftedness is not an occupational title. Many people nowadays identify themselves according to what they do for work: "I'm a lawyer, salesman, homemaker, student," and so on. But I would point out that before you are an occupation, you are a *person*. What you happen to be doing for a career may fit your personhood—but you are not your job.

BUT WHAT ABOUT . . . ?

By this point, I know I've raised a thousand questions: Where does giftedness come from? If it's inborn, then what about the influence of one's environment? What about people with disabilities or mental issues? What about genetic factors? How does giftedness relate to personality? This sounds intriguing, but where's the science for it—the research, the numbers, the control studies? If everyone has giftedness, then why do so many people hate their jobs? If I have my giftedness, why can't I figure out what to do with my life? By saying giftedness is about what people enjoy doing, aren't you just giving them an excuse to live self-indulgently? And what about people living in poverty? Is giftedness just a luxury? What if it turns out someone doesn't like their giftedness? How can giftedness be instinctive when people spend their whole lives becoming who they are?

> Each of us is meant to be a gift to others, if we use our gifts appropriately.

In addition, you may be asking more practical questions like: How can I find a job that fits me? I already know what I want to do, so how can I get paid to do that? How can I get along better with my boss and/or coworkers? My child has learning differences; do you have any advice on dealing with that? How can I help my twentysomething son or daughter decide on a career? I want to get married, so how do I find the right person? Now that my kids are grown up, what can I do that will be meaningful and satisfying? How can I make my life count?

So many questions! You can see why, when I'm at a party or a dinner and someone asks what I do, I often end up being the center of attention for a while, answering questions about giftedness. People find this stuff fascinating. So did I when I first heard about it years ago.

That's because giftedness is all about the one thing we all care about the most—ourselves. But not in a self-absorbed way. Rather, giftedness opens up a way to talk about ourselves that actually takes us outside of ourselves. We not only discover that our giftedness is a gift to us but a deeper truth—that each of us is meant to be a gift to others, if we use our gifts appropriately.

How you read this book and what you do with it is totally up to you. But I would point out that how you learn about your giftedness will itself be driven by your particular giftedness. Because that's you. That's how you do life.

I want to honor that. Indeed, I want to celebrate that! That's why I wrote this book. I believe there is something important you were put here to do—something *only* you can do. As Steve Jobs said shortly before he died, "Your time is limited, so don't waste it living someone else's life."

I couldn't agree more. But if you don't know what your giftedness is, you're liable to do just that.

WHAT IS THIS THING CALLED YOUR "GIFTEDNESS"?

You don't want to be living someone else's life. And you don't have to, because your giftedness is a remarkable thing! An amazing thing! You may not feel that way about it yet, but my job is to help you see what is already inside of you and unleash it for the benefit of the world.

In this chapter I'm going to describe the nature of your giftedness and what makes it so special. But remember, in talking about giftedness, I'm really talking about *you*.

ONE SIZE FITS ALL?

The idea that people differ from one another is hardly new. From the Montessori Method to Howard Gardner's theory of multiple intelligences to Marcus Buckingham and Donald Clifton's *Now, Discover Your Strengths*, which launched the popular StrengthsFinder online assessment tool, the emphasis on individuality is now firmly entrenched in popular culture. Companies selling products as varied as jeans, coffee, hamburgers, investment opportunities, running shoes, and computers encourage customers to tailor their purchases to their own individual tastes and preferences.

However, our world is still a long way from embracing or honoring the vast implications of human individuality. Most schools in the United States and throughout the world still educate people as if we all learn in the same way. Most workplaces still manage people as if we all thrive under the same form of management. Most employers still reward and compensate people as if everyone is motivated by the same incentives. Many cultures around the world still operate under centuries-old traditions that reward conformity and discourage individuality.

Even in our personal lives and relationships, most of us still buy into ideas that run counter to the idea that people are unique. For example, how many books on marriage have you read that claim men think one way, women think another way? In other words, all men are alike, and all women are alike. That doesn't sound very unique to me.

When it comes to parenting, countless books inform parents about the developmental stages and characteristics of children. But suppose your child deviates from those "norms"? Why, then they need to be checked out! There must be something wrong with them! Because, of course, the underlying assumption of "norms" is that all children are pretty much the same. (Any mother who has more than one child intuitively knows that children are absolutely *not* the same.)

There's no question that humans share many things in common. Among those things is giftedness, but even when two people have a similar kind of giftedness, they turn out to be two very different people.

Albert Einstein was like Warren Buffett in that he displayed a keen interest in numbers and mathematics from an early age. When Einstein was an adolescent, a tutor gave him a copy of Euclid's classic text *Elements*. He devoured it, calling it the "holy little geometry book." At seventeen he enrolled in a mathematics and physics program at the Zurich Polytechnic Institute.

Do you see the similarities between Einstein and Buffett? Both were incredibly precocious with numbers. To that extent, they were very much alike. But Einstein steered his mathematical bent toward physics, while Buffett ended up in investments. The more you study the two men, the more unique each of them turns out to be—even if they share a great deal in common.

YOUR GIFTEDNESS IS ABOUT WHAT YOU'RE BORN TO DO

Giftedness is not about what you can do but what you were born to do, enjoy doing, and do well.

People *can* do all kinds of things. But they only enjoy doing certain things. And I'm not just talking about what people "like" to do—fun activities like throwing a dinner party, mountain climbing, lying on the beach, going to movies. Yes, some people do end up making careers out of those activities. But when they do, what do we say about them? "Wow, that person was born to do that!"

When I say "enjoy," I'm talking about a genuine sense of motivational satisfaction. Everyone has something they gain energy from doing.

For one person, it may be solving a problem. They never met a problem they didn't like to solve. Maybe they do jigsaw puzzles or Sudoku. Maybe it's the problem of keeping their twenty-five-year-old car running in pristine condition. Maybe it's the problem of organizing their work group for better effectiveness. Maybe it's the problem of filling in critical gaps in their family's genealogy. The problems may vary, but what matters is that that person looks at the world as one giant set of problems to solve. And when they finally do solve a problem, they have that feeling of, "Yes!!! I got it! I figured it out! I fixed it! I solved it! I saw the answer! I got it running again."

> The giftedness is not in the activity itself, it's in the person, in their sense of joy or fulfillment or accomplishment.

But notice: the giftedness is not in the activity itself, it's in the person, in their sense of joy or fulfillment or accomplishment. They are solving problems instinctively. They were born to solve problems—at least, things *they* see as problems, regardless of whether others perceive things that way. It's just what they naturally do.

Those of us who make a career out of studying giftedness have a saying: *Nothing of consequence happens in the world apart from people gifted to the task.* No symphony has ever been composed, no war has ever been won, no invention has ever been invented, no mountain has ever been scaled apart from people (sometimes individually but most often in teams) with the right combination of strengths and motivations to do what is required to produce greatness.

You can always spot someone who is "gifted to the task." They just exude a sense of enjoying what they're doing. And they're good at it. The results are pleasing. And we're impressed with what they've accomplished.

You can see people gifted to the task in everyday accomplishments, but sometimes their gifts play out on a grand stage. Take Martin Luther King Jr. delivering his "I Have a Dream" speech to the March on Washington in 1963. Or recall the crew of Apollo 13 and the Mission Control team that safely returned the spacecraft after it suffered a catastrophic explosion as it neared the Moon in 1970. Or attend a Cirque de Soleil performance with its theatrical blend of circus arts and music. All such accomplishments are the result of people who are gifted to the task.

So it is with you. There is something you are born to do. That thing may never place you on the world stage. But that's immaterial. What matters is the realization of your own personal greatness, the thing you were placed here to do. Your giftedness is the best, and I daresay the only, means you have of making your greatest contribution to the world. And trust me, no matter how simple or seemingly inconsequential your giftedness turns out to be, it *does* have the potential for greatness!

YOUR GIFTEDNESS IS ABOUT HOW YOU FUNCTION

Giftedness is fundamentally about your behavior. It is found in *what* you do and *how* you do it.

Not so much *why* you do it. The question of why is interesting, but in the end it can only end up in speculation.

For instance, I could tell you about a woman who loves to plan things. She's been planning things since she was a little girl: planning daily activities, planning birthday parties as a youngster, planning her study schedule as a high school student, planning events for her church youth group, planning a campaign for a friend running for student government in college, planning her wedding, planning her daughter's nursery, planning family vacations, planning her financial future. You get the picture.

Whatever else you can say about that woman, she loves to plan. And she's good at it. She was born to plan.

Why does she plan? Is it because her mother was scatterbrained, so she had to take charge from an early age? Is it because her father was an engineer with a methodical, rational manner? Is it because her parents accidentally left her behind one Sunday when they drove home from church, and she was traumatized by the uncertainty? Is it because she has a certain gene that is somehow associated with logical, predictive, risk-averse tendencies?

No one can say for sure why this woman plans. But one thing is certain: she loves to plan. That's what really matters. By leaving it at that, we are able to stick with easily observable data from her own life history, not speculation as to what might have happened long ago and far away, or might be happening deep inside her now.

Remember, giftedness is a phenomenon. It just is. I can ask why the phenomenon of giftedness itself exists and where it comes from. But when it comes to an individual—including you—I don't ask why you have the giftedness you have. I simply observe your behavior and then describe you accordingly, because your behavior—the consistent pattern of what you actually do and how you do it—tells me what your giftedness is.

YOUR GIFTEDNESS IS ABOUT YOUR CORE STRENGTHS AND NATURAL MOTIVATION

Giftedness is about behavior, but not just any behavior. You may do any numbers of things, but certain activities have a way of focusing your energy in a highly engaging way. If you examine those moments carefully, you'll discover a consistent intertwining of strengths and motivation in your behavior.

Many assessments look at abilities (sometimes called aptitudes or talents or capacities or skills). But a person is not necessarily *motivated* to use all the abilities they have. I've met people who had significant musical ability, but no motivation to pursue anything related to music. Likewise, I've worked with people who had unusual athletic ability who nonetheless had no interest in participating in sports.

Conversely, we all know people who love to sing in the shower, but we're very glad they don't sing in the choir at church! They have no ability to sing. And of course, countless American men would kill to be able to throw a football like Tom Brady or Peyton Manning. But they simply don't have that ability, no matter how motivated they might be to do that.

Giftedness is a marriage of ability *and* motivation.

The good news is, everyone has some combination of both. Perhaps it's the motivation and ability to bake the perfect soufflé. Or mill a piece of steel to just the right specifications. Or handle the complexities of guiding a jetliner to an airport. Or successfully negotiate a deal that everyone else thought was dead. Or figure out how to communicate with an autistic child. Or create an imaginary world that causes readers to suspend their disbelief.

> I almost never use the word "passion" in my work, because I think it's a red herring.

You have a combination of motivation and ability that enables you to do something rather unique and special. You may have no clue as to what that is, but it's there and it can be discovered.

By the way, when I say "natural" motivation, I mean motivation that comes from within. Cultures use many external motivators to get people to do things: fear, money, sex, envy, guilt, shame, pain. Those can be powerful motivators, for sure. But they introduce energy from the outside.

Giftedness springs from within—not what you have to do or are coerced to do but what you love to do.

It's what drives the fortysomething career woman to go ahead and run the marathon she spent evenings and weekends training for, despite having bronchitis and a sore knee, in thirty-four-degree weather with sleet starting to fall. No one's paying her to do that. No one is forcing her to do it. She does it because something inside says, "I *want* to do this! I *must* do this! I will not have it any other way!"

Again, it's what keeps the researcher up all night, poring over his data and calculations, determined to find the answer to the question he's been pondering for months. He gets paid the same whether he goes to bed at 9:30 or not. But it's not his paycheck or his boss driving his behavior. It's him! He's the one who will not rest until he's solved the riddle.

Every person is naturally motivated to seek some unique, intensely satisfying outcome. If you tap into that core drive, you unleash the wellspring of their energy as a human being.

Now let me clarify what I mean by what you "love" to do. Some readers will assume I'm talking about passion. It's all the rage nowadays to urge people to "follow your passion." But I almost never use the word "passion" in my work, because I think it's a red herring.

Passion is an emotional response to something that moves you deeply. Some people have a pretty wide emotional bandwidth, so they're just "passionate" by nature. They're passionate about their work, their family, their dog, their community, their sports team, their church. Golf, chocolate, country music . . . you name it, they're passionate about it!

Most other people, however, have a much narrower experience of emotionality. Even if something moves them, they rarely feel much passion about it. So when they hear, "follow your passion," they're in a bind, because they don't feel particularly "passionate" about anything.

That's why I prefer the term "motivation." *Everyone* has some form of intrinsic motivation, and we can find out what that is by observing them using it.

YOUR GIFTEDNESS NATURALLY INCLINES TOWARD SATISFACTION AND PRODUCTIVITY

If giftedness is about motivation combined with ability, it follows that it is also about satisfaction combined with productivity. When you get to do what you're motivated to do, you feel satisfaction. And if you do what you're actually able to do, you tend to be productive. You accomplish something.

That's what makes giftedness so valuable in the workplace. We need people to get stuff done in this world! It may be the manufacture of a widget or the completion of a sale. Or the outcome may be "softer," like the education of a student or the composition of a song. But work at some level has to create value. It has to end up making the world a better place in some way. If it doesn't, no one wins.

> People are not machines. They are looking for something that feeds their souls.

But then we discover that people are not machines. You can't just set them to a task and expect them to carry out that task until you unplug them. No, people have something inside them that demands satisfaction. They of course work for a paycheck, because they have to feed their families and pay their bills. But people are actually looking for rewards in their jobs that go way beyond the monetary. They are looking for a *pay-off*, something that feeds their soul.

A woman came to see me who was a senior executive in a corporation. She had been promoted several times until reaching her current position. Most people would say she had reached the pinnacle of success. So why was she coming to me?

"Because I have got to find something more fulfilling," she declared. "I'm dying where I am! I took this job because they didn't have anyone else to take it, and they needed someone with experience and a long history with the company. So I agreed. They doubled my salary when I took the job and they've doubled it again since. If I asked, they'd probably pay me whatever I wanted."

Then she blurted out, "But it doesn't matter, because I can't do this anymore. I love the company. I love the people. But I'm no longer getting anything out of the job. It's slowly wearing me down. I've got to make a change."

That woman was at the height of her career in a leadership position at a world-class company. By all measures, she had reached the top. But as Jim Collins perceptively notes, "It is impossible to have a great life unless it is a meaningful life. And it is very difficult to have a meaningful life without meaningful work."[1]

I must add a disclaimer that some people actually do derive a great deal of satisfaction from making money. Those folks often end up being very successful in business, particularly as investment bankers, insurance representatives, venture capitalists, oil wildcatters, and similar careers. Certain kinds of giftedness thrive on coming out ahead, and they use profit as a means of keeping score.

Judging by the thousands of assessments I've seen over the years, I estimate that only about 25–30 percent of the population is fundamentally motivated by money or to work with money. Yes, again, people need to get paid—and most of us think we should be getting paid more than we are. But money is not in the motivational equation for most people. Not in terms of the work itself.

And you can see that when you study people's giftedness. For example, I frequently work with college students and young adults who possess sheer brilliance in terms of creative potential or leadership or analytical ability or athletic talent. They can become absolutely transfixed when engaged in whatever their "thing" is. But you'll search in vain to find any real interest or motivation to be bothered with money. The money part is almost a distraction. It never enters their consciousness when they're in the zone of their giftedness.

"Then how in the world are they going to make a living?!" I hear someone (like a parent) ask in exasperation. In truth, that's also the question they're asking.

> **The being/doing distinction is a false dichotomy.**

I'll address that in chapter 7. My point here is that we humans possess a longing that no amount of money can ever satisfy. But what does satisfy it is the achievement of that uniquely personal, motivational payoff we are constantly seeking. That quest ultimately drives our behavior.

YOUR GIFTEDNESS INVOLVES BOTH BEING *AND* DOING

Reading that giftedness involves what you *do* will raise an alarm for those who subscribe to the adage, "Who you are matters more than what you do," or "It's not what you accomplish that counts but what sort of person you are."

For those folks, describing people and their personhood in a doing-based way may seem terribly dehumanizing. It makes it sound like people are mere machines, constructed for utilitarian purposes and otherwise devoid of meaning.

Well, if that's what giftedness were all about, I would reject it out of hand. But giftedness is as much about being as doing, and in fact reveals that the being/doing distinction is a false dichotomy. Giftedness shows that "who you are" is meaningless apart from "what you do," because what you do expresses who you are.

I sigh every time I hear someone trot out the chestnut that "we're called human beings, not human doings." Nonsense! It's impossible to know who someone is until they do something. You can insist all day long that you are patient. But it's only when you smile and say kind words to the grocery checker after spending twenty minutes waiting in line that I have any basis to conclude, "Wow, she's a remarkably patient person." Conversely, if you melt down and start giving the checkout person a rather nasty piece of your mind, then I will conclude, "No, she's really not patient at all."

Either way, doing expresses one's being.

Think of the biography of Warren Buffett. Biographies by their nature attempt to answer a "being" question: *Who is/was this person?* They do that by telling stories that show the person in action—what they do and how they do it. By that means, we come to understand how the person sees life, what matters to them, how they handle conflict or adversity, what things they take advantage of, what their strengths are, what characteristics they lack, who they need around them in order to flourish, and of course what they accomplish.

The best way to understand a person is through story. Every human is an actor in a dynamic narrative that is playing out over time. So if we want to understand any given person—including you—we have to know your story. And the secret is to look at things you yourself have *done.* Chapter 5 and the exercise in the back on "Discovering Your Giftedness" will explain more about that process.

YOUR GIFTEDNESS IS FINITE AND FOCUSED, YET BRIMMING WITH POSSIBILITIES FOR EXPRESSION

For as long as I've been helping people figure out what to do with their life, I've confronted a dilemma. On the one hand, given endless possibilities for what a person could do, people want me to narrow things down to the one thing they ideally should do. On the other hand, if I told them, "Okay, here's what you should do," they would push back and say I'm putting them in a box. (By the way, I never tell you what you can or can't do with your life; I simply provide information for you to make that choice.)

> It's very freeing to be able to say no to things you shouldn't be doing.

Giftedness has a wonderful way of avoiding either pitfall. At one and the same time, it focuses you while widening your options.

Let me explain by way of analogy. Let's say that a hammer doesn't know it's a hammer. In other words, it doesn't know what it was designed to do. Lacking that knowledge, it's liable to go around breaking windows, putting dents in cars, or trying to drive screws. Talk about a misfit! Worst of all, it may smash a thumb, because a tool that doesn't know what it was designed to do is not only a confused tool and foolish tool but a dangerous tool as well.

But now, suppose someone helps that hammer understand that it was designed to drive nails? Suddenly the prospects for meaningful work enlarge dramatically—because there are so many nails in the world. From then on, that hammer won't be looking for a job, it will be looking for nails.

The same holds for you. You are uniquely wired to do something. By pinning down what that something is, you can eliminate all the stuff that doesn't fit you and focus on what does.

It's very freeing to be able to say no to things you shouldn't be doing. For example, the born problem-solver I talked about earlier no longer has to wonder where he should focus his efforts. He now knows he should look for "problems" he can solve. Those problems can come in a wide variety of possibilities (and the specifics of his giftedness, along with his background, education, experience, etc., will invariably pare down the options). Meanwhile, he can steer clear of situations that are, by his standards, problem-free.

Likewise, the lady who loves to plan can keep an eye out for opportunities to plan. She can let others teach, build, perform, lead, write, coach, negotiate, sell. In fact, she may prove invaluable to those others in helping them plan out how they will accomplish what they are wired to do.

Sadly, some of us have bought into the myth of omnicompetence, the idea that we're supposed to be good at everything. We may have been told that we can do anything we put our mind to, and we believe it. But such is not the case. We are all limited by our giftedness—by whatever our core "thing" is.

But the good news is that your core thing has endless possibilities for expression and application. Which is very good news if you need to change careers. Your giftedness is not occupation-specific. It can be applied in many fields.

One of my clients was an elite swimmer throughout his teens and twenties. He won world records and eventually turned pro. But at thirty, he realized he was ready to do something else. Fortunately, his giftedness was not in his swimming but in him. At heart, he is a man on a quest for a grand adventure that he can document in some way. So imagine all the possibilities that insight opens up for someone who has a great reputation, a wide network, maturity, health, and resources. But at the same time, it steers him clear of occupations that would stifle his curiosity and cause him to grow restless.

The "portability" of giftedness has profound implications for you if you are nearing the end of an especially successful career or assignment. It's commonplace for such people to rest on their laurels and go around identifying themselves as "the former athlete," "the former CEO," "the former senator," or whatever. Likewise, it's common for such people to start settling for relatively inconsequential roles—serving on boards, making after-dinner speeches, being a celebrity spokesperson, etc.

I think that's a huge waste of giftedness. If you've hit the top in your career, it's probably because that field made good use of what you were born to do. So why "retire"? Why not redeploy your giftedness into some other area that could use it—especially if it means a more sophisticated use of your giftedness?

Former President Jimmy Carter is a great model of doing that. He arguably has accomplished more since he was president than while he was president. Since leaving office he has established the Carter Center, which works on behalf of human rights and the alleviation of suffering. The center is credited with eliminating more than 99 percent of guinea worm disease. Carter has also intervened to resolve conflicts and/or promote justice in countless countries worldwide. In 2002 he received the Nobel Peace Prize for the work he has accomplished since his presidency.

Regardless of your opinion of President Carter's viewpoints and strategies, you can't deny that instead of just sitting back and coasting, he has applied his giftedness to some very challenging world problems.

YOUR GIFTEDNESS IS PRESENT FROM YOUR EARLIEST YEARS

The stories of Warren Buffett and Albert Einstein show how their fascination with numbers showed up at a very early age. That kind of precocious activity is commonplace in observing people's giftedness.

My friend Jerrie Moffet, who's been teaching first grade for thirty years, told me about a young orphan whom one of her colleagues encountered in the slums of Haiti. Before he was old enough to start school, he began stealing radios, cell phones, calculators, and other electronics. Needless to say, he became the bane of his village. But further investigation found that he was not selling the equipment or using it for personal gain. He delighted in taking the devices apart in order to figure out how they worked. Someone had the bright idea to encourage him in that activity instead of punishing him for it, and soon the boy developed a thriving cottage industry fixing broken electronics.

I recall an interview I had with a preacher who remembered a favorite activity from when he was two-and-a-half years old. He and his brother and sisters would play hide-and-seek for hours, until dusk was falling and their mother was calling them to come inside. The only noteworthy detail he could remember about that activity was that he always wanted to be the one everyone was looking for, not one of the seekers.

An analysis of numerous activities from that man's life revealed that his giftedness was all about getting people to respond to him—a good match for a career that consistently places him onstage. In a way, his story of hide-and-seek is a kind of metaphor for his life: he was born to have people looking for him.

I can offer countless cases of people like that preacher, showing that giftedness appears at a very early age. My own opinion is that it is present from birth.

I certainly saw that with my three daughters. I was in the birthing room for all three of their entries into the world. I promise you, right there on the weighing table each of them manifested themselves in three completely different ways. And that hasn't let up since!

I realize I'm raising the whole nature-versus-nurture debate about human development: Are children hardwired from birth, or do the influences of their environment determine who they "become"?

I'm not a developmental psychologist, but my work with people's giftedness convinces me that humans come into the world with the core of their personhood already intact. Immediately upon birth (though actually, while still in the womb), that personhood begins to interact with the environment, and especially the people it encounters: parents, siblings, schoolmates, teachers, coaches, love interests. Some of those interactions are fortuitous in that they honor the personhood of the individual. Others are rather conflicted and even damaging. All have an influence. But all of those influences are working on something that is hardwired. They do not "make" the person. At best, they shape the person. But they do so in ways that heavily depend on the nature of the individual's inherent personhood.

So let's say that five-year-old Jennifer takes an interest in the piano, and before long her mother has her taking piano lessons. She practices. She enjoys playing music. She's good at it for her age. Will she grow up to be a concert pianist? The answer is: it all depends on Jennifer. It all depends on what her giftedness is about.

One form of giftedness is about mastering something and honing it to perfection. If Jennifer is driven by that, she may well end up practicing in a seemingly obsessive way, because she won't quit until she's got the piece down perfectly. If life cooperates and she's able to study under better and better teachers, and if she gets into a top-tier music school, and if she's encouraged to enter the right competitions, and if she's offered guest performances at the right venues—then yes, she may well become a professional concert pianist. But her interest—and I emphasize *her* interest—is not really to be a concert pianist, it's to play perfect music.

> Many, many things will change over the course of your life—but not your giftedness.

Meanwhile, a different form of giftedness has to do with learning new things and then showing you can do them. If Jennifer is motivated by that, she may end up practicing quite diligently and performing well at her recitals. That cycle may persist well into her teen years. But then one day Jennifer encounters an entirely new activity, riding horses. Suddenly she is keen to take lessons in that, and her interest in the piano may wane. Once she's in college, yet another subject, biology, may capture her interest. So she might delve into that with abandon. To some, Jennifer may appear to flit from one thing to another. But her behavior is rather consistent: she keeps laying hold of one new learning adventure after another.

I caution parents to beware of trying to "lock in" on what your child's giftedness is and then plan their future to fit your conclusions. I'll say more about recognizing your child's giftedness in chapter 8. For now, just ponder the fact that your child is already a person with his/her own giftedness—just like you when you were their age. Whoever raised you likely ran the gamut from honoring your giftedness to overlooking it to blocking it, because they probably knew nothing about giftedness. But by now you do! Armed with that advantage, you can be a great parent for your child.

YOUR GIFTEDNESS IS ENDURING

Having shown up at an early age, your giftedness remains stable and never fundamentally changes throughout your life. I'm aware that popular thinking takes it as a given that we humans are always changing and "becoming" different people. We're constantly "evolving," as the saying goes. But actually we're not.

Many, many things will change over the course of your life: your knowledge and understanding, habits, values, relationships, jobs, interests, concerns, beliefs and convictions, likes and dislikes, tastes and preferences, vocabulary, possessions. Your body will certainly change!

But your essential giftedness never changes. It does develop, but it doesn't turn into something else. Likewise, where and how you express your giftedness may vary widely. But the core strengths and motivation you were born with will remain stable throughout your life.

Consider John James Audubon, the great painter of birds. Born in 1785 in what is now Haiti, he was the son of a French naval officer and his chambermaid. Almost from the beginning, Audubon displayed a love of birds. "I felt an intimacy with them," he said, "bordering on frenzy [that] must accompany my steps through life."[2]

Audubon's father recalled that the boy "would point out the elegant movement of the birds, and the beauty and softness of their plumage. He called my attention to their show of pleasure or sense of danger, their perfect forms and splendid attire. He would speak of their departure and return with the seasons."[3] Growing up in France, Audubon spent a great deal of time in the woods, collecting birds' nests and other treasures, which he would then painstakingly draw.

When Napoleon came to power, Audubon's father shipped him off to the United States. He lived with a group of Quakers, writing that "hunting, fishing, drawing, and music occupied my every moment; cares I knew not, and cared naught about them."[4] He developed methods for banding birds, painting and drawing them, and stuffing them for display. By chance he met a professional ornithologist who introduced him to the scientific study of birds.

Audubon married, and soon he had a family to feed. He tried his hand at various businesses, but one by one they failed. Finally he declared bankruptcy and was thrown into debtors' prison. He sadly commented, "My heart was sorely heavy, for scarcely had I enough to keep my dear ones alive." And yet, "through these dark days I was being led to the development of the talents I loved."[5]

Most people trying to emerge from bankruptcy look for the fastest, surest, safest way to get their finances on a stable footing. Not Audubon. Leaving his wife to do the best she could to provide for the family, he packed his gun and paint box and headed south on the Mississippi River. His goal: to track down and paint all the birds of North America and turn them into a book.

He succeeded in finding and documenting the birds. But when he went to find a publisher, he was met with scorn by the scientific community. He might have quit had he not run into Charles Bonaparte, nephew of the French emperor. Bonaparte suggested that Audubon's work might find a more receptive audience in Europe.

Armed with little more than that faint hope, he set off for England in 1826 with three hundred drawings. Bonaparte's instincts were dead-on. The Brits adored Audubon's documentation of the States and quickly agreed to publish his work under the title *Birds of America*.

Several years ago I was privileged to attend a private showing of *Birds of America* at the Dallas Public Library. The work is in two volumes and contains 435 hand-colored, life-size prints of 497 species of birds. Every one of them is a work of art. A year or so after I saw those volumes, they sold at auction for $2 million. Not bad for someone who at one time sat in debtors' prison!

Why did Audubon keep coming back to his relentless interest in birds? Some would say he had determination and persistence. I would agree. Some might say he was just plain silly and impractical, and only through luck managed to get his work published late in his life. Meanwhile, he and his family suffered tremendously. Was it really worth it? I think if we had Audubon here today, he would say it was absolutely worth it.

But again, what kept the fire burning in his soul? As I said earlier, we can have all kinds of debates about the why. What is beyond debate is that Audubon's fascination with birds and their depiction remained a lifelong compulsion.

Giftedness is enduring. It springs up early and outlasts changes of employment, changes of relationships, changes of obligations and commitments, and changes of scenery. As the poet William Wordsworth noted, "The Child is father of the Man."[6]

YOUR GIFTEDNESS CAN BE DEVELOPED

Your giftedness never fundamentally changes, but that doesn't mean you can't develop as a person. Indeed, your giftedness is your most powerful tool for personal and professional growth, and that in two ways: (1) you can develop your gift itself, and (2) you can use your gift to acquire skills and cultivate competencies that you did not come by naturally.

Before explaining that, let me deal with the common myth that personal development is primarily about overcoming your weaknesses. In a way, I don't really believe in the concept of weakness. Some personality assessments give you a list of your strengths ("here's what you're good at") juxtaposed against a list of your weaknesses ("here's what you need to work on"). I reject that distinction out of hand.

I believe that people are like tools in that they each have a certain design that fits them to do a certain function. A screwdriver, for instance, is the perfect tool for driving screws. If you use it for that purpose, it works like a charm. And if the screwdriver could talk, it would likely say, "I love it when you use me to drive screws." Driving screws is the essential strength of a screwdriver.

But now, imagine that I say to the screwdriver, "You do a beautiful job driving screws, but you have a real weakness driving nails. You should work on that." That would be nonsense!

Yet we do that all the time with people. We say, "Charlie, you're a great salesperson, but you have a real weakness for managing people." We level that criticism (for that's what it is), having never bothered to consider whether Charlie has any intrinsic motivation, predisposition, or interest in managing people. Maybe Charlie has been placed in a job where managing people needs to happen, but that's a problem of placement, not a problem with Charlie.

> **What keeps someone at a task for ten-thousand hours?**

You excel when doing the thing you were born to do. Your strength is in doing that thing. Anything beyond that is, at best, a limitation or a lack of strength, but not a "weakness."

Peter Drucker said, "One cannot do anything with what one cannot do. One cannot achieve anything with what one does not do. One can only build on strength."[7] If you want to grow, develop, and contribute, focus on your strengths, not your weaknesses.

Which brings us to developing your giftedness itself. To do that, you first must know what it is. But having identified it, you can then cultivate and mature it by feeding it with education, experience, opportunities, tests and challenges, and as much as anything, intentionally exercising it over time.

Psychological research shows that people who end up at the top in any field get there as a result of one thing: they work harder than everyone else. In fact, much harder—ten thousand hours harder, to be exact. It's called the ten thousand Rule.

According to neurologist Daniel Levitin: "The emerging picture [from the research] is that ten thousand hours of practice is required to achieve the level of mastery associated with being a world-class expert—in anything.... In study after study, of composers, basketball players, fiction writers, ice skaters, concert pianists, chess players, master criminals, and what have you, this number comes up again and again."

Then Levitin makes this intriguing disclaimer: "Of course, this doesn't address why some people get more out of their practice sessions than others do."[8]

That's a good question. A great question, actually. From the standpoint of human motivation and how we choose to spend our lives, perhaps it's *the* key question: What keeps someone at a task for ten thousand hours?

I believe I know the answer. The only way you'll do something for ten thousand hours and be productive at it is if you're gifted to that task. The activity has to tap into the deepest part of your core energy and reward you with some sort of meaningful satisfaction. Otherwise you won't stick with it. You may be forced to stick with it (e.g., if your parents won't let you quit, if you have to make a living doing it, etc.). But your heart won't be in it. And there will be too many temptations to quit and too many obstacles to surmount to hang in there for years on end.

But what if you do find something that fits you and devote ten thousand hours to it? Levin says you'll end up at the world-class level. Imagine: within you there is something that has world-class potential. Wouldn't you like to discover that gift and develop it?

That's really "all" that happened for Warren Buffett. By sticking to his knack for numbers and the concept of compounding, Buffett developed an extremely sophisticated use of his giftedness.

The same can and should happen for you. Like Buffett, there is something in your heart of hearts that you "just want to do." You may not be interested in making a living with it. But that ought not to be your primary concern. Rather, what are you doing to develop that gift? Are you even aware of what it is? If so, are you better at doing it now than you were a year ago? What could you do in the next twelve weeks to honor that gift and feed it in some practical way?

In addition to feeding your gift, you can use it to grow and develop. For example, let's say you want to learn a new language. There are countless ways to do that. Which of them would be best for you? Your giftedness answers that question, because it dramatically affects how you learn.

Are you someone who learns best through a structured, ordered process that supplies lots of guidelines and instruction? Then you might find that a formal language class would be the best approach. Or perhaps you're more independent and like to work at your own pace. Then an online language course might be the way to go. Or maybe you're someone who always does things in partnership with others. Then you'd probably benefit from inviting one or two friends to learn the language with you.

I had a client who told me about a required course in international studies that he had to take in order to graduate from college. He put it off until the second semester of his senior year, as he had no inherent interest in that subject. But he had no choice.

As he pondered how he could get through the semester, he realized that the professor's tests were all based on facts and information easily obtainable from the course's textbook. If he knew that stuff, he could pass the course. He had excellent powers of memorization (I think he was a theater major). So he devised various rhymes, lyrics, acronyms, and other wordplays to remember the material. By that means he consistently scored well on the tests and earned a B+ in the course.

Did he actually learn anything about international studies? Well, you wouldn't want him in the State Department. But he took great pride that long after college he was still able to name all the countries of the world as of 1982. That ought to count for something!

YOUR GIFTEDNESS IS SOMETHING YOU INSTINCTIVELY USE

When you use your giftedness, you don't think about using it, you just use it. It's natural. It's instinctive. You wouldn't think of doing life any other way.

The purpose of this book is to help you become *intentional* about using it. But I want to point out that it's actually good news that you don't think about using it. That simplifies life. Giftedness is not an expectation you have to live up to; it's an expression of who you intrinsically are. As Master Yoda tells Luke Skywalker in *The Empire Strikes Back*, "Do. Or do not! There is no try." Giftedness is natural. There's no need to be self-conscious about it.

If everyone had to know what their giftedness is in order to use it, the world would be in a bad way. Fortunately, enough people seem to end up in jobs that allow them to express their giftedness that we all benefit from their genius, even though they may have little or no idea of what they are contributing.

Take Winston Churchill. When he was a boy, Winston had thousands of toy soldiers in his room. He spent hours arranging those lead pieces into battle formations, his mind imagining various scenarios and devising various campaigns.

One summer the Churchills rented a house in the country, where Winston and his brother, Jack, built a log castle, complete with a moat of water, over which a drawbridge could be raised and lowered. The boys proceeded to prosecute a siege, with mud and rocks flying.[9]

Those scenes from Churchill's childhood illustrate the precocious nature of giftedness, which I mentioned earlier. But they also show the instinctive nature of the phenomenon. At some core level, Churchill was born to strategize in warfare. No one taught him to do that. No one made him do it. He instinctively did it. He could not *not* do it.

> At some core level, Churchill was born to strategize in warfare. No one taught him how to do it.

And how fortunate for everyone living in Western civilization today! Because across the English Channel from young Winston was another little boy living out the instinctive nature of his giftedness. For whatever reason, his gifts turned dark and menacing. That boy organized gangs of toughs in his neighborhood and drilled them in military fashion. He had a way of feeling things deeply and communicating passionately and persuasively. But he also tended to hold grudges and feel as if the world had mistreated him. In time, he, like Churchill, rose to ascendancy in his country, where his evil was unleashed in full force, igniting a world war and the calculated slaughter of millions.

Giftedness has consequences. You can't just leave it at the level of instinct, unexamined and unmanaged.

On the other hand, you can't manufacture giftedness. You can't "make" yourself have a certain kind of giftedness. No one can teach it into you. You can't buy it. You can't engineer it. You can provide it with education, but education is not the origin of it—because giftedness is instinctive. So, the best thing to do is identify it and then honor it.

YOUR GIFTEDNESS IS IRRESISTIBLE
AND IRREPRESSIBLE

Hand-in-glove with the notion that giftedness is instinctive is that it is irresistible, in that you cannot deny it, and irrepressible, in that you cannot suppress it.

My appeal is for the open expression of giftedness, because I've seen too many cases where someone has tried to block or rein in either their own giftedness or someone else's. A classic case would be Tyler, the class clown at his middle school. Students and teachers alike know from long experience that Tyler will do just about anything to get a reaction from his peers.

But then in ninth grade, Tyler goes to high school and meets Mrs. Page. She's an old-school educator who doesn't suffer fools gladly. When Tyler pops off a duck call in response to a classmate's erroneous answer to a question, Mrs. Page pulls him out into the hall and tells him in no uncertain terms that such behavior will not be tolerated. The next time he disrupts the class, he'll be sent to the principal.

> No matter how harsh or hostile the environment, a person will seek out ways to unleash the energy that is within them.

Not surprisingly, Tyler makes a lot of trips to the principal that year. Because he can't help himself! He can try to suppress his innate sense of humor. Mrs. Page can threaten him all she wants. But sooner or later, the perfect moment will come along, and no amount of effort or resistance in the world will stop Tyler from impulsively blurting out the quip that has suddenly entered his mind.

Tyler's giftedness is irresistible and irrepressible. He cannot *not* express it.

There's a fascinating film, *Twenty Feet from Stardom*, which documents the harsh realities of the women (mostly African American) who sang backup vocals, beginning in the 1960s, for the likes of Aretha Franklin, Ike and Tina Turner, Lynyrd Skynyrd, Luther Vandross, The Rolling Stones, Sting, Bruce Springsteen, and countless other superstars. One of the women featured in the film is Darlene Love, who wrote the classic "Christmas Baby (Please Come Home)." Her producer, Phil Spector, intended his wife, Ronnie, to sing that song on a Christmas album he was putting together. But when Ronnie proved unequal to the task, Spector called in Darlene Love to record it instead. Then when the album came out, he credited his wife as the artist.

Darlene Love continued to sing backup into the mid-1970s. Then she left the music industry to raise her family. She had no savings and was receiving none of the royalties from the countless hits she had recorded over the years. Deeply depressed and practically broke, she ended up cleaning houses to make ends meet.

Then one day during the Christmas season, she was at a customer's home when she heard a familiar tune on the radio: "Christmas Baby (Please Come Home)." It was her song! Her voice! Somehow that moment spoke to the deepest part of her and reawakened her soul. In a flash she realized: "I *must* sing! I *must* go back!" And so Darlene Love returned to the music scene—not to try and be a star (though eventually she did meet with success and was inducted into the Rock and Roll Hall of Fame in 2010). But fame was not her aim. She simply had to express that which she could not hold silent. Her giftedness *had* to out!

Giftedness *always* seeks expression. No matter how harsh or hostile the environment, a person will seek out ways to unleash the energy that is within them.

My colleagues and I have worked with people who came from extremely negative backgrounds: abuse of all kinds, poverty, lack of education, abandonment, war and loss, and other traumas. Despite such horrific conditions, their giftedness not only survived but found ways to express itself, even if defiantly.

In Cateura, Paraguay, is a slum built on a landfill. Residents scavenge the garbage to meet their basics needs and find materials to recycle. Yet even in this desperately poor community, someone has the idea that children should have music. So people with a knack for making things begin fashioning crude but surprisingly serviceable musical instruments from the trash. One creates a cello made from an oil can, scraps of wood, and discarded kitchen implements.

Another forms a violin out of plastic and cardboard. He says, "I never imagined myself building an instrument like this, and I feel very happy when I see a kid playing a recycled violin."

A girl who plays the instrument says, "When I listen to the sound of a violin, I feel butterflies in my stomach. It's a feeling that I don't know how to explain."

Someone else organizes the young people into an orchestra—a "recycled orchestra" named Landfillharmonic. They practice. They study music. They perform the classics. And they delight in this new form of self-expression. One girl says, "My life would be worthless without music."

The orchestra conductor says, "People realize that we shouldn't throw away trash carelessly. Well, we shouldn't throw away people, either."[10]

I couldn't have said it better myself.

> **Your giftedness does not have an expiration date on it. As long as you're alive, it will be trying to express itself.**

The irresistible, irrepressible nature of giftedness is fantastic news for you if you grew up in difficult circumstances. You *do* have giftedness! Your background has not robbed you of that, even if it has left you with many wounds and scars. If you will make the effort to identify that giftedness and put it into play, you will discover the best of who you are. You will also find a triumph of your spirit, because nothing proves more satisfying than living out your giftedness.

YOUR GIFTEDNESS IS INEXHAUSTIBLE

Many of my clients are creative people whose minds are like Roman candles shooting out an endless stream of ideas for projects they want to do: videos to make, paintings to paint, songs to write, events to stage, dinners to host, etc. A common fear is that their creative juices will suddenly stop and they'll run out of ideas.

They needn't worry, nor should you. Your giftedness does not have an expiration date on it. As long as you're alive, it will be trying to express itself. You'll never wear it out no matter how many times and ways you use it. It's like your eyesight: no matter how many things you see in this world, you never tire of seeing.

YOUR GIFTEDNESS IS MORALLY NEUTRAL

Giftedness is inherently good but morally neutral. That is, it can be used for both good and evil. I'll say more about that in chapter 9.

But just consider this: the worst ills that humans commit do not spring from their so-called weaknesses but rather when they use the full power and weight of their innate gifts for selfish or evil purposes. 9/11 took a great deal of giftedness to pull off. The Holocaust required a significant amount of giftedness to orchestrate. Such horrors rarely come about by accident.

Remember the phrase I gave earlier: nothing of consequence happens in the world apart from people gifted to the task. While that applies to humanity's greatest and most noble achievements, it also applies to their worst and most despicable.

I suppose we could create a rogue's gallery of individuals and groups whose gifts were given over to dark ends—people like Ponzi scheme artist Bernie Madoff, or Ken Lay of Enron, or mobster Al Capone, or mass murderer Charles Manson and the Manson Family, or cult leader Jim Jones, or the Colombian drug cartels, or the white supremacist prison gang Aryan Brotherhood, or the Bloods, Crips, and other gangs that infest America's cities. The list goes on and on.

When you think about how much trouble folks like that have brought on the world, it's staggering to imagine what they could have accomplished if they had applied themselves to better and more life-giving purposes. It's also a cautionary tale for all of us: What's the potential for you and me to wreak havoc on others through the inappropriate or malicious use of our gifts?

YOUR GIFTEDNESS IS RELIABLE BUT NOT INFALLIBLE

Would you walk across Niagara Falls on a tightrope? How about the Grand Canyon? Nik Wallenda has done both. He's able to do death-defying feats like that because he's got natural-born strengths for doing so. It's also true that he practices relentlessly, stays in tip-top shape, plans his stunts in infinitesimal detail, and prays a lot.

Now I could practice, train, plan, and pray, too. But I doubt I'd stay on a tightrope for twenty-two nanoseconds, let alone the twenty-two minutes, fifty-four seconds it took Wallenda to cross the Grand Canyon. That's because I don't have the strengths Wallenda has. I have other strengths, but not those.

When I talk about strength, I'm talking about something you can rely on in the moment of truth. When a surgeon slices open a chest to do open-heart surgery, she's relying on her strengths related to surgery that enable her to do the job. Again, she's trained those strengths, given them experience, teamed them up with other people's strengths, and (hopefully) says a prayer before she starts cutting. But she expects her strengths to show up when the procedure begins.

So it is with the strength of your giftedness. You can rely on it. You can trust it. It's what allows you to perform the way you're capable of performing.

> Your giftedness has a way of showing up for you even when you don't feel so good.

This aspect of giftedness is a huge advantage for us as humans, because let's face it, as Scott Peck put it so well, "Life is difficult."[11] It is indeed! Most of us are just trying to get through the day, and we have all kinds of stuff pushing against us: traffic jams, colds, spills, crying babies, dysfunctional bosses, lazy coworkers, incompetent clerks, parking tickets, indigestion. As Woody Allen is said to have quipped, "Most of the world's work is done by people who don't feel so good."

And yet . . . your giftedness has a way of showing up for you even when you don't feel so good. In fact, exercising your giftedness has a way of reenergizing you when you don't feel so good. It's a huge boost physically, mentally, and emotionally.

I saw that time after time in my dad. I'd watch him get off a plane Monday evening absolutely spent from an entire weekend of speaking and traveling. He'd go home and fall into bed, utterly exhausted. But at 6:00 the next morning, he'd be up and raring to go teach a class of students. It didn't matter if he had a stack of bills, a sick child, a broken washing machine, and undone chores at home. He was on fire to go teach! Teaching energized him that much. Teaching had a way of canceling out all that negative energy in his life.

One further piece of evidence that giftedness can be counted on is that it yields results even when someone knows they didn't do their job as well as they could have or should have. Again, I can remember my dad coming home and openly berating himself for being "off his game" in some talk he had given. I mean, he'd be ashamed of himself! Later I'd come across someone who had attended that same presentation, and they'd exclaim, "That was the best talk I've ever heard your dad give!"

That's the power of giftedness. Even when you turn in what for you seems like a B- or C+ performance, if you're operating in your sweet spot, others are liable to award your efforts with an A+. Because to them what you've done is impressive.

There's just one significant caveat: the reliability of your gift can be a blessing, but it's not a carte blanche. You can trust the gift to show up, but you can never presume on it to show up. You can't coast and say, "I don't need to study. I don't need to practice. I don't need to expend energy. I'm gifted to the task, so all I have to do is show up."

When people do that, they fail. And they often fail at the worst possible moment. Because giftedness is not infallible. It arms us with strength, but it doesn't make us superhuman. Nor does it defy the laws of the universe. The teacher may be brilliant, but he's liable to fail the student that needs insight rather than an impressive lecture. A lady may be a genius at planning, but the one domino she misses could bring down the entire operation. Someone may be the best salesperson ever, but the day they knock off early will turn out to be the day their competitor steals their biggest client.

It appears that God has made us humans strong, but fallible. No doubt that's why Nik Wallenda always says a prayer before he takes his first step across a chasm.

YOUR GIFTEDNESS AFFECTS HOW YOU SEE THE WORLD

In fifth grade my mother took me for my annual visit to the eye doctor (whose name, believe it or not, was Dr. Stare). After having me read an eye chart on the wall, he dilated my eyes, turned down the lights, and pulled down a contraption that had big dials on it and two eyepieces for me to look through. He then put up the eye chart again and began turning the dials.

As he did so, the image on the wall got sharper or fuzzier. He'd get into a rhythm of asking, "You like *theez* (that's how he pronounced "this")?" Click. "Or *theez*?" I'd answer. Click. "Theez?" Click. "Or *theez*?" I'd answer. Click. "Theez?" Click. "Or *theez*?" I'd answer. After a while he turned up the lights, filled out a prescription, and handed it to my mother.

A few days later I went back to school wearing a new set of glasses. And my world looked completely different! I could see again.

From the time you were born, you've been wearing a set of glasses that radically affects how you see the world. You pay attention to certain things and not to others. You see events in a particular way and interpret them accordingly. You see things other people don't see, and you miss things other people notice. You keep looking at certain things longer than others do. And you "connect the dots" between certain events that never occur to other people.

In short, thanks to your giftedness, you literally see the world in your own unique way. And when I say "see," I mean that broadly in terms of perceptions and what you pay attention to, regardless of which sense you use.

This past week I read about a little boy who isn't even past the third grade and is already one of the best "ear" birders in his part of the country. That means he can identify bird calls by simply hearing them, and in fact can distinguish between normal singing and distress calls. He can even tell when a bird is mimicking another species. When his mother asked him how he could do that, he told her, "When you listen to an orchestra, can't you tell the difference between the trumpet and the piano?"[12]

We all speak a different language by virtue of how we're wired. And it's not just that various occupations each have their own special jargon. At the individual level, we each speak our own unique dialect.

That makes for some interesting communication, to say the least. Which brings us to . . .

YOUR GIFTEDNESS AFFECTS YOUR RELATIONSHIPS

I've devoted all of chapter 8 to giftedness and your relationships. But for now let me tease you with my premise that most of the conflicts we have with others originate from our different ways of seeing the world.

Remember the Tower of Babel?[13] The people begin a building project all speaking the same language. God is not pleased with their plans, so He confuses their language and the project falls apart and is abandoned.

Well, something similar happens when even two people start interacting. It doesn't matter how compatible they are, sooner or later there's bound to be a misunderstanding. Sometimes they talk it out and discover that one of them saw things one way; the other saw things rather differently. But sometimes their miscommunication leads to far more serious outcomes.

If for no other reason, you do well to know something about giftedness in general and yours in particular because of the way it affects all of your relationships.

YOUR GIFTEDNESS CAN BE "PLUSSED" BY THE GIFTEDNESS OF OTHERS

If your giftedness has such a profound impact on your relationships, it follows that when it's combined with other people's giftedness, it can be significantly enhanced and benefited. Indeed, what happens may border on the spectacular.

That's the genius of the modern corporation. The collective strengths of an organization quantitatively multiply what any one person could accomplish on their own. Even relatively small teams can achieve blockbuster results and create unprecedented value (consider the team that started Facebook; or the team of seventy, led by Dr. Ben Carson, that was the first to successfully separate conjoined twins in 1987; or a team of Navy SEALs). Whatever the potential of a single person's giftedness—which is absolutely enormous—the power of combined giftedness is almost beyond imagining.

YOUR GIFTEDNESS DOES NOT EXPLAIN EVERYTHING

No matter how amazing your giftedness is or how far-reaching its implications, it is but one of countless factors affecting how you behave, what choices you make, and what ultimately happens in your life. When it comes to you, giftedness is a core factor, but not the only factor.

Human beings are exceedingly complex. The human brain alone is the most sophisticated system yet known, but our study of it is still in its infancy. Then there's the rest of the body, where, too, we've only begun to scratch the surface.

Alongside that material dimension is the immaterial nature of people—our souls and spirituality, our relationships (especially families and lineages), our emotions and psychology, our societies and cultures, our moral categories, our economic and political choices, the lifelong process of learning and development, communication, language, creativity, music, art. On and on. There are doubtless dimensions within us and around us that we're still not even aware of.

So I don't want to leave the impression that giftedness answers every question in your life, any more than genetics, or brain theory, or psychology, or birth order, or philosophy, or any other single category answers every question. Any expert in any field who makes such a claim is simply simplistic.

So that's my disclaimer. But now in the same breath, let me reiterate that while your giftedness is not all that's involved in the things you do, it's involved to some degree in everything you do, because it's tied to your personhood. So the more you can know about it, and about how it works, the more insight you'll have into the things that matter most to you—like who you are, why you're here, and what you should do with your life.

I've already talked a lot about who you are. In the next two chapters let me turn to the larger question of why I believe you and I are here.

THE GOOD TRUTH ABOUT YOU

Artist Andy Warhol famously observed that "in the future, everyone will be world-famous for fifteen minutes."[1] With the advent of YouTube, Twitter, and the omnipresent camera phone, that quip moves ever closer to realization.

All of which begs the question: When your fifteen minutes arrive, what will you be famous for?

Many times I've found myself in an embarrassing predicament and thought, "Well, I sure hope this won't end up being my fifteen minutes of fame!" Because in this day and age, if one of your worst moments ends up being what you're remembered for, fifteen minutes of fame could well translate to a lifetime of shame!

THE "BAD TRUTH"

Ironically, however, I find that many people actually focus most of their attention on the worst parts of their lives. When they ponder the question, *Who am I?*, they primarily see themselves through their deficiencies: their pathologies, dysfunctions, addictions, learning disabilities, personal tragedies, weaknesses, mistakes, sins . . . you get the idea.

I certainly wouldn't discount any of that stuff. It's undeniable. Humans do things and have things done to them that are just awful. And without question, we all have "issues." I call those dark realities the "bad truth" about a person.

Sadly, the "bad truth" is where lots of people house their identity. Which is one of the main reasons I wrote this book. I think it's time to pay a little more attention to the "good truth" about you. And your giftedness is *very* good truth! Sure, it has a potential dark side to it, as we'll see in chapter 9. But at heart, it's an inherently positive, affirming, and laudable phenomenon.

In fact, it's a downright inspiring phenomenon! That's probably why I'm so captivated by it. Giftedness pushes me to find and, if possible, unleash the *best* of who a person is.

Am I just a Pollyanna, an overly optimistic dreamer who instinctively tries to see the best in people? Most certainly not! If you could read my mind sometimes, you'd definitely conclude that I'm anything but that.

WHERE DOES GIFTEDNESS COME FROM?

No, I think what most exhilarates me about giftedness is how we got it. You see, I don't believe we are here by chance. I know some do, and that's fine. But I actually do believe there's a God, and that He's responsible for all of us being here. (Never mind the question of how He's done that. That's a different discussion.)

> Most people instinctively want their lives to matter.

There are many narratives to account for how humans came to be. But one of the main reasons I side with the narrative that says God made the world and the people in it is because it seems to fit the facts and experience of my specialization, which is human giftedness and motivation, better than any of the others. As I want to show, viewing giftedness as an endowment from God has a way of compelling people to believe that they matter. It inspires them toward a vision for their lives. They have a reason for being here.

I mean, if I truly thought that I'm just a product of random chance, I'm pretty sure I'd end up saying, "Well, then, it doesn't matter how I live or what I do. In that case, I'll make it all about me. Because nothing matters anyway. I'll just look out for me, and grab as much as I can get in life that suits me."

I see a lot of people today living with exactly that mindset. It's an outlook rooted in cynicism. Those folks may or may not be finding the personal satisfaction they seek, but all-about-me-ness certainly governs their life.

And yet I find that most people instinctively want their lives to matter. If they thought it were actually possible, they'd like to live with a sense of significance, purpose, meaning, and direction. Apparently you do, or else you wouldn't have picked up a book subtitled *Why You're Here, Why You Matter & What You Should Do with Your Life*.

So what if I can show you from your own life history that, from birth, you have indeed been seeking to live out a unique purpose that you find personally fulfilling and meaningful? That would at least be something. You might or might not accept my premise for where that purpose comes from. But that's okay, I've got pragmatism on my side: what I'm offering "works" regardless of where it comes from.

STITCHED TOGETHER

As I've explained, giftedness is an undeniable part of the human condition. It's common to all, yet unique within each individual. Do we find a narrative anywhere that describes the source of this universal yet intensely personal energy?

Yes, we actually find many. One of them is in a poem (originally a hymn) in the Old Testament. In that poem, David reflects on how God knows him intimately and is present with him constantly, right from the very beginning of his existence:

For you created my inmost being;
    you knit me together in my mother's womb.
I praise you because I am fearfully and wonderfully made;
    your works are wonderful,
    I know that full well.
My frame was not hidden from you
    when I was made in the secret place,
    when I was woven together in the depths of the earth.

Your eyes saw my unformed body;
all the days ordained for me were written in your book
before one of them came to be.[2]

While most translations only hint at it, these Hebrew lines are composed of a poetic mashup of images that include the body, an artisan, the womb, and the earth. God is portrayed as a master craftsman who is weaving, knitting, or embroidering a garment or tapestry. He is making something—a person. And He is intimately involved in every step of that process.

My first wife, Nancy, loved to quilt. She died of breast cancer in 2000. But over the years we were married, she probably put together six or eight quilts, along with several unfinished pieces. Creating a quilt was a huge production. First she had to come up with an idea. Then she went around to all the fabric stores to find colors and patterns that fit her concept. She measured out all the pieces and carefully cut them to size. She arranged them in a pattern. She spent hours sewing the pieces together, painstakingly careful to make each stitch look exactly like the others. Then she took the assembled top to a place where they added the batting and attached the backing and did a lot of other things I had no clue about.

Having finished the quilt, Nancy was ready for the part she loved most—presenting her creation to the person for whom she made it. Perhaps to a friend or family member as a Christmas present. Or to one of our daughters as a keepsake. What made these unveilings so special was that in each quilt there was something of the person, but there was also something of Nancy. The quilt was as much a stitching together of souls as it was of fabric.

David says that God stitches together a person. In doing so, He not only makes a new person, He expresses something of His own personhood. Because that's what artists do: artists and their art are inseparable.

YOU ARE DESIGNED

The final two lines of the passage read, "All the days ordained for me were written in your book / before one of them came to be." The word "ordained" means "formed" or "fashioned." Interestingly, that same word is used in Genesis 2, where we also find an account of God making a human being—namely, Adam. Verse 7 describes God "forming" Adam out of what most versions translate as "dust." But it's legitimate to think in terms of mud or clay,[3] and to see God fashioning Adam like a piece of pottery.

Another of Nancy's hobbies was ceramics. She used to go to a workshop that had different kinds of clay and a potter's wheel and a kiln. She spent hours there "throwing" pieces of pottery. It was very physical, hands-on work to mold the clay into a bowl or a plate or a cup or whatever. It was also messy: as she turned the piece on the wheel, the lubricating water would fly off, and Nancy would come home with splatters of mud on her face and in her hair. She loved it!

That's what I picture when I read Genesis 2—God getting His "hands" into the mud in order to fashion Adam. He is not dictating Adam into being; He is totally absorbed in handcrafting him. What results is not only a person but God's fingerprints on that person.

Back in Psalm 139, we could also use the word "design" to translate our term in the next-to-last line: "All the days *designed* for me were written in your book." We'll revisit that line later. For now, I just want to emphasize that Psalm 139 goes to the heart of what I call the "good truth" about you: *You have been designed by God from the womb.*

Now if that's true, then when should that design start showing up? From the womb! Not three years, five years, twelve years, or twenty years after you've been parented, educated, socialized, and whatever else to "become" whoever you're supposed to be. No! That design should be in evidence from the start.

And so it is. The phenomenon of giftedness begins to manifest itself from a person's earliest days—in my experience, right from the womb. When I see an infant who shows feisty determination grow into a toddler who will not be denied, and then into a child with a strong will, and from there into a teenager who loves to place himself in contests of fortitude and strategy, and finally into an adult who takes on challenge after challenge after challenge, I can only conclude that her bent for challenges was present when she came into the world.

In short, the phenomenon of giftedness appears to dovetail with what the Bible says about how God designs a person from the womb.[4]

SO WHAT?

So why is that significant? Well, for one thing, if that's true, it means you are not random. You are not here by chance. Your existence is not just nature's capricious roll of the dice. Your presence on the planet is neither luck nor a mistake. Someone put you here. Someone intentionally thought through who you should be and carefully worked to bring that concept into reality. That alone invests you with intrinsic dignity and value.

But it means so much else! For one thing, it means your giftedness is from the hand of God. It shows the fingerprints He left on you when He made you.

Perhaps you've heard the idea that humans are made in the image of God. That comes from the creation narrative in Genesis 1: "Then God said, 'Let us make man in our image, in our likeness. . . .' So God created mankind in his own image, in the image of God he created them; male and female he created them."[5]

> When God looks at you, He sees Himself in a way He sees in no one else.

It's common to think of being made in the image of God as something that's generically true about humanity as a whole. People will say, "We're all made in God's image," meaning that everyone has dignity and value, and so we should treat everyone as a child of God.

I don't disagree with that. But giftedness boosts our understanding to a whole new level. "The image of God" is not just some amorphous designation that applies generally and universally. No, it's intensely personal! It applies to *you*. And when we look at your giftedness, we discover how you *uniquely* bear God's image. In other words, when God looks at you, He sees Himself in a way He sees in no one else. How incredible!

For that reason, I call giftedness "incarnational truth." That is: when God designs a human being, He takes some dimension of Himself that He does in an infinite way and fashions a human being to do that exact same thing, only in a finite way. So when a person does the thing that God has designed them to do, they mirror for the rest of us a dimension of God that we otherwise would never get to see.

For example, consider the person who loves to build things and create finished products. God does that same thing. Indeed, God is building things and creating finished products before that person ever exists. God is doing that in an infinite way (because God is infinite). But then God places that person into the world and fashions her with a set of core strengths and motivation for building things and creating finished products—just like He does. As a result, we find her building things and creating finished products. As she does, God delights in her activity, because He sees a treasured dimension of Himself in her very being.

What do you suppose your own giftedness is all about? Is it to bring understanding and insight to other people? To introduce structure and order into messes? To use food and other means to create an unforgettable experience for others? To have adventures that test your mettle and get your adrenaline going? To quietly enter into the experience of a struggling person in order to bring encouragement, support, and understanding? To have others pay attention to what you say or do? To take care of animals? To keep the grounds of a college campus shipshape?

Whatever your giftedness is, you are doing something God has been doing since before you ever existed. He's designed you to resemble Him—to "image" Him—in that particular way. When you do that thing, you honor God. You bring Him what is called "glory." And He delights to see you reflecting something of Him in human form.

The story of Eric Liddell, dramatized in the film *Chariots of Fire*, describes this much better than I can. Liddell grew up in the early twentieth century. He felt called to be a missionary to China, so he attended Oxford and then Edinburgh to prepare. He was known to be very fast, so he was recruited to Great Britain's 1924 Olympic team.

In the film, Liddell's sister, Jenny, is alarmed that her brother might forsake his calling to China, and she nags him about it constantly. Finally, to set her mind at ease, Liddell invites her to take a walk. Along the way he turns to her and says, "Jenny, you've got to understand. I believe God made me—for a purpose. For China. But He also made me fast, and when I run I feel His pleasure!"[6]

That may be the best expression of giftedness I've ever heard: "God made me fast, and when I run I feel His pleasure." Eric Liddell never met a race he didn't want to run. No one taught him that. If anything, his sister felt she needed to discourage him from doing that. But he was just born to race. He could not *not* do it. And when he did it, he could "feel God's pleasure." What a fantastic summation of what it's like to live out the image of God!

The same thing applies to you. God has placed something inside of you, such that you could say, "God made me _____, and when I do that thing I feel His pleasure." You may have no clue what that thing is. But I assure you, it's there. It's there even if you don't believe there is a God, or that He made you. There's a delight that rises up inside you whenever you get to do a certain thing that's unique to you. I believe that thing is there because you have been made in God's image, and you are mirroring what God does. He takes infinite delight in seeing you do that thing.

WHAT? GOD DELIGHTS IN ME?

Is it hard to accept the notion that God delights in you? I'm afraid for many people, it is. As I mentioned earlier, they're constantly dragged down by the "bad truth" about themselves. They feel so messed up that they conclude, "I'm not good enough for God. Somehow He's got to be angry at me. I hear He loves me and all, but still, He probably doesn't think too much of me."[7]

I think that mindset is actually one of the main reasons some people ignore God or try not to think about Him very much, or even say they don't believe in Him. Who wants to believe in God if He's basically mad at you all the time, and you feel like you can't measure up?

I'll come back to that in a moment. But I want to stick with my premise that God delights in you. David certainly realized that God had done something delightful when He put him together: "I praise you because I am fearfully and wonderfully made; / your works are wonderful, / I know that full well."

Plenty of people nowadays think they are fearful and wonderful—but not the way David means. I'm thinking of various celebrities on image platforms like Hollywood or the NFL or MTV. They strut around boasting about how "bad" they are, fairly intoxicated with their own self-importance. They have a gift or a talent, and they act as if the world should bow down and worship them for it.

Not David. He's not making a statement about himself but about God. He's reflecting on the nature of his own being and how it all came together, and he ends up in awe of his Maker. His praise is directed toward God, not himself.

And yet within that praise, he describes himself as "fearfully and wonderfully made." He acknowledges the delightfulness of God's finished product. I suppose we could paraphrase that delight this way: "Oh, my gosh, I really am awesome! I'm amazing! I'm just unbelievably special and unique! God, what You have made takes my breath away. I'm filled with wonder and amazement because of You. I never could have imagined You would make something so profoundly delightful. It's beyond what I could have asked for, but just what I would have always wanted."

When's the last time you looked at yourself and cried out, "I praise You, God, because I am fearfully and wonderfully made"? David says he knows that "full well." Do you? If not, you would do well to devote more attention to reflecting on what God had in mind when He put you together. Let me see if I can help.

THE THOUGHT IN GOD'S MIND

Remember those last two lines from the Psalm 139 passage? "All the days *designed* for me were written in your book / before one of them came to be." David realizes that when God looks at him, He sees the entirety of David's life at a glance, from birth to death. In fact, God sees even more than that: "Your eyes have seen my unformed substance." That means when David was just an embryo, a seemingly chaotic mass of tissue inside his mother's womb, God was there watching him. So that adds another nine months to the "days" that God has "written" for David.

But is that the sum total of God's awareness of David—nine months of gestation plus however many years between David's first cry and final breath? Hardly! Before David ever existed, before he was conceived and born, before he had done anything good or bad, David was on God's mind.

The same is true for you. Before you ever came to be in this world, you were a thought in God's mind.

That's huge! The thing you have to remember about God is that He sits outside of time in eternity. Eternity is hard for us to grasp as finite humans. We live in time. But there is no time in eternity. No past. No present. Only now. An eternal now. God dwells in that eternal now.

Believe it or not, that's to your advantage. It means that whatever God is or does is eternal. So if He has a thought of you, that thought is eternal.[8] It never ends. In fact, it's never started. He's always been thinking about you. More correctly, He always thinks about you.

Ponder that: whether or not you ever think about God, He's *always* thinking about you.

God is also good. Not just good the way we often think of "good," meaning "good enough" or even "really good." But perfectly good. Infinitely good. The very essence of good. There is nothing in God that cannot be good. Which means that every thought of His is good. Including His thought of you, which He is always thinking. You are a perfectly and infinitely and eternally good thought in God's mind.

God eternally has you on His mind.

Moreover, God is perfect love. Infinite love. Eternal love. So whatever thoughts He has, those thoughts express His love and include that which He loves. In addition, He loves all of His thoughts. God's thoughts are so perfectly good that He can only love them. He can only be delighted in them. He cannot have a thought in which He does not take delight.

Applied to you, all of that adds up to a very astounding premise—that you do not actually begin when you are born, nor even at the moment of your conception. You begin, ultimately in the mind of God. Before you exist in time and space, you are an eternal thought in the mind of God. There is never a time when God is not thinking of you and then suddenly has the idea of you. He *always* thinks about you.[9]

I know I may be stretching your imagination here, but work with me. God eternally has you on His mind. It's as if there's a "space" inside God that only you (that is, His idea of you) and He inhabit. In that space, you are His only thought. How special is that!

What's more, He is absolutely delighted with that thought. Out of His extravagant love, He has dreamed you up, just the way He desires. And that dream, that idea, that person whom God sees in His mind's eye in some way reminds God of Himself. And since God is perfect and good and loving and praiseworthy and a thousand other infinitely noble qualities, what He sees when He imagines you fills Him with delight, because He delights in Himself. He sees Himself in you. In some small, finite way, you are what God would look like if He were to appear in human form.

Now let me be clear. You are not God. You are not divine. You are not infinite, or eternal, or perfectly good in and of yourself, or self-sustaining, or all-powerful, or all-knowing, or omnipresent, or any of the other attributes that characterize God. You are a thought in God's mind—until, that is, He renders you with His own "hands," fashions you with your particular giftedness, and places you in time and space. At that point, you display for everyone to see—but most importantly for God to see—some unique aspect of God.

So Shakespeare was right. The world is indeed a stage,[10] and you're one of the actors in its drama. But ultimately your performance is not only for the benefit of the other people onstage but for the audience of One. God gets to see you live out one of the endless dimensions of His own Being. Your story fits into the plotline of the human story, which in turn fits into the far greater story line of what God is up to.

BUT WHAT ABOUT THE "BAD TRUTH"?

By now, some readers will be beside themselves because I'm describing humans in such lofty terms that I'm practically making us sound like gods,[11] when the truth is, we're such a mess and have made a mess of the world. Just look around today. Could anyone seriously argue that humans have not brought the planet to the precipice of disaster? Can we really say that the world as it is would be what you'd expect from creatures supposedly made in the image of God?

At the personal level, I've already pointed out that many of us feel our lives are such a mess that we could never believe that God thinks much of us.

So we come to a mystery. In the biblical narrative, the same humans who are said in one place to be "made in God's image" are at the same time declared elsewhere to be universally "corrupt" and "abominable." We are told that none of us does good. None of us seeks God.[12] Our giftedness fits us to bring God glory, yet we're told that all of us "fall short of the glory of God."[13] God somehow is always thinking of us, yet we're written off as "dead in [our] trespasses and sins."[14]

David himself—the same David who exulted, "You knit me together in my mother's womb"—later wrote, "I was sinful at birth, / sinful from the time my mother conceived me."[15]

How can this be? How can you and I mirror God Himself and yet be so terribly and tragically messed up? How can that good truth and bad truth coexist in one and the same person?

THE PERSON ON GOD'S HEART

I don't pretend to understand it. But three things seem clear. One is that no matter how corrupted you and I may be, before we ever exist and before we ever do anything good or bad, we are on God's mind. And God *delights* in that person whom He sees in His mind! He cannot do otherwise, for in us He sees Himself.

Which goes a long way toward explaining a second, deeper mystery that Christians have celebrated for two thousand years—that God took on human form, lived the life He intended for us to live, then submitted to an undeserved death, and in doing so dealt with our "messed-up-ness" so that we might yet realize the vision He had in creating us.[16] In other words, God treasures us enough to reclaim us.

Is any of us good enough for God? Well, of course not, but that's not really the point. What matters—indeed, what is decisive—is that God values us. God desires us. God thinks we are special. Each of us is one of God's favorites.

If you ponder that thought enough, you eventually end up where David did: "I praise You because I am fearfully and wonderfully made."

Again I ask: When's the last time you've said that to God?

The fact that it is even possible to say that to Him brings us to a third profound reality: God is personal. He is not a force or an energy field or some amorphous, universal spiritual state of being. He is a Person. In making you He has not made a thing or even an animal but a person. In that way, too, you are made in God's image.

What is a person? That's been a question of long and spirited debate. I won't dive into the depths of that subject here. But I will say that if humans are indeed designed by God—by whatever means God does that—our understanding of what it means to be a person must take into account the personhood of God. Each of us has our own unique personhood only because we received it from the Person who put us here.

Why did that Person make you as a person? Because He desires a relationship with you. That's what persons do—they relate to one another. God did not give you your personhood in order to ignore you, abandon you, forget you, or cut you off. Quite the opposite. He desires to know you and be known by you, and you by Him. You're always on His mind and heart.[17] In fact, you're always in His presence.[18]

So anytime you want it, you can have an actual relationship with God. There's nothing holding Him back. That was the whole purpose behind Jesus' life, death, and resurrection. He dealt with the "bad "truth" about you, so now nothing stands between you and God.

If you seek a relationship with Him, it will be a real relationship. By which I mean, your experience of God will be totally different than anyone else's, because He has made you thoroughly unique. By virtue of your giftedness, God will interact with you in ways He doesn't interact with anyone else. To God, you're not just another face in the crowd, another mouth to feed, another number on a list. God delights in you as a person with a name. Indeed, whatever you were named at birth or go by now, God knows you by your true name. The more you pursue Him, the more you come to know your true name, too.

YOUR PURPOSE, YOUR POWER

In *The Lion, the Witch, and the Wardrobe,* there is a scene in which Peter, Susan, and Lucy, along with Mr. and Mrs. Beaver, are overtaken by Father Christmas (Santa Claus). The bearded elf pulls out gifts from his bag for each of the children: to Peter a sword and a shield; to Susan a bow, a quiver of arrows, and a horn; and to Lucy a dagger and a vial containing a healing cordial. After distributing these gifts, Father Christmas declares, "These are your presents, and they are tools, not toys."[1]

So it is for every one of us. Each human being has been given a gift, and our gift is a tool, not a toy. It is intended for use, and not merely for our own pleasure—although as we have seen, our gift by its very nature can bring us a great deal of pleasure, satisfaction, and joy.

YOU AND YOUR "GOOD WORKS"

In the last chapter I argued that your giftedness has intrinsic value because it shows that God has designed you from the womb. But your giftedness also has instrumental value in that God has given it to you for a purpose.

In a New Testament passage that parallels Psalm 139, we read, "For we are His workmanship, created in Christ Jesus for good works, which God prepared beforehand so that we would walk in them."[2]

This verse doesn't use the term *giftedness*, but it offers a similar concept in the word "workmanship." The word means a "made thing" or "crafted thing." Just as Psalm 139 uses the image of a tapestry or garment being woven together, here we have the same idea of something being handcrafted. Since God is the One whose "hands," so to speak, are doing the crafting, the end result is a masterpiece. It's beautiful. It's spectacular. It's genius.

You are God's masterpiece. That alone makes you intrinsically valuable.

But now, let's dig a bit deeper into the meaning of "workmanship."[3] In first-century Ephesus, artisans made things like pottery, jewelry, leather goods, dishes, musical instruments, and the like. So when we read this passage, we can imagine an Ephesian potter at his wheel, fashioning something from clay.

If the potter fashions the clay one way, the finished product is perfect for holding wine or water. If he fashions it another way, it's perfect for holding grain or bread. If he fashions yet another way, it's perfect for holding oil and a wick and using as a lantern.

The way the potter designs the workmanship fits it for a particular task. The unique design features give it functionality, and that introduces the idea of purpose. Which is why the verse goes on to say you have been "created in Christ Jesus *for* good works" (emphasis added).

I suppose most of us think of "good works" as acts of charity: feeding the homeless, caring for orphans, helping little old ladies across the street, that sort of thing. Well, those are certainly good works and they ought to be done.

But in light of the word "workmanship," the "good works" mentioned in this passage are not just generic good works but rather specific good works tied to the nature of the workmanship. Which means if we can figure out your workmanship (how you've been designed), we can go a long way toward discovering what sort of "good works" you are born to do.

And just like Psalm 139, this verse says that all of this was prepared "beforehand," which means in eternity, that you would "walk in them," or live them out.

Boiled down to plain English, this passage tells us that from eternity God looks out on the twenty-first century and sees certain "good works" that He wants done. To get them done, He dreams up a person—the person we now call by your name. At just the right moment in time and space, He renders you with His own "hands," outfitting you with just the right combination of strengths and motivation to be the perfect "tool" to accomplish those good works.[4]

In short, you've not only been designed by God from the womb, *you've been placed here for a purpose.* You have a destiny. God has work for you to do. He's assigned you a task with your name on it.

Now can you see why I'm so intent on helping you find out what your giftedness is? Because unless you appreciate the nature of your "workmanship," you really have no way of determining what you should devote your life to. You're just flying blind when it comes to choosing a path.

Again, C. S. Lewis says it better than I can: "The first qualification for judging any piece of workmanship from a corkscrew to a cathedral is to know what it is—what it was intended to do and how it is meant to be used. After that has been discovered the temperance reformer may decide that the corkscrew was made for a bad purpose, and the communist may think the same about the cathedral. But such questions come later. The first thing is to understand the object before you: as long as you think the corkscrew was meant for opening tins or the cathedral for entertaining tourists you can say nothing to the purpose about them."[5]

The same could be said for you: the first thing we need to know about you is what you were *intended* to be and to do. Once we figure that out, it's infinitely easier to come up with a meaningful answer to the question: *What should you do with your life?*

> The world lies fallow until human beings do something.

GIFTEDNESS IS ACTUAL POWER

As we've seen, Psalm 139 likens you to a garment or tapestry that God has woven together. Ephesians 2 likens you to a piece of pottery that God has formed for a purpose. Those images are beautiful. Nonetheless, they are somewhat benign. They make you sound like an object of functional art—something to be admired and used, like a plate of Lenox china or a Ferrari.

But you are not art, you are a person. Yes, you are a "made thing," but unlike all other things, God has crafted you to be a "maker" of things. That's in large part what it means to be made "in God's image." You are like God in that something He does in an infinite way, you are designed to do in a finite way. In short, your giftedness arms you with power to do something in the world, something of real consequence. Your gift is indeed a tool, not a toy.

Return with me to Genesis 1, the narrative of God creating people in His image. Immediately upon doing so, He pronounces a blessing on us: "Prosper! Reproduce! Fill Earth! Take charge! / Be responsible for fish in the sea and birds in the air, / for every living thing that moves on the face of Earth."[6]

We humans are charged with the privileged assignment of taking charge of the earth and making it fruitful. On its own, the world is not fruitful. It only yields natural resources—not 2 x 4s, rebar, gasoline, concrete, electricity, automobiles, computers, chocolate ice cream, button-down shirts, pianos, fireworks, ebooks, or Wii. The world lies fallow until human beings do something.

We call that something work. Work is actual human energy that has an effect on the world, including other people. Work is essential to being human, and it was bestowed by God as a blessing. Later, of course, a curse created serious consequences for work. But work itself remains a blessing on humanity. It's how God provides for our needs. He's given us the earth with all of its incredible resources,[7] and our work makes that earth productive.

That includes the most productive and valuable resource of all, human capital. Knowledge work has tapped into the deep reservoirs of human giftedness with results that go beyond anything people a thousand years ago—or even 150 years ago—could have imagined. And we're only seventy years or so into this new development!

Whatever your giftedness is, it arms you with the power to have an effect on the world. That effect may be to invent something. To explore new territory. To secure capital. To design a tool. To manufacture a product. To sell goods and services. To ensure quality. To organize the work itself. To fly an airplane. To keep track of money. To negotiate a deal and its terms. To create a policy. To enforce the law. To protect ownership. To grow food. To understand a species of animal. To educate youth. To take care of people's bodies. To lead or manage a team. To create art. To tell stories. To disseminate information. To provide entertainment. To minister to people's souls. To delve into the meaning of things.

There are as many possibilities for work as there are humans. But we are all included in the mandate to prosper, reproduce, fill the earth, take charge, and exercise responsibility for the world. Each of us has been given our giftedness in order to play our particular part in the dominion granted to humanity, which at heart was established as a blessing upon the earth.

And that giftedness involves actual power. It has an actual effect on the world. You can see that throughout history in the numerous feats that humans have accomplished: the building of the pyramids, the Great Wall of China, the circumnavigation of the world by Magellan, the invention of movable type, the Suez Canal.

But it's been through the wide-scale flourishing of knowledge work following World War II that we've seen the most far-reaching displays of the enormous power latent within human giftedness. When communities of people are educated, organized, free to explore and innovate, resourced by capital, allowed to share in the profits, and able to communicate widely, the sky literally seems to be the limit on what can happen.

Every time an airliner lifts hundreds of thousands of pounds off a runway, the giftedness of thousands of people is on display. When a surgical team separates a pair of conjoined twins, the giftedness of countless professionals is involved. When a company that sells chicken sandwiches becomes the second-largest quick-service chicken restaurant in America by using cows as its chief marketing theme, human giftedness can be found behind that brilliant counterintuitive strategy. The means by which 1.3 billion people can access a simple platform for social interaction anytime of the day or night has come about through lots of people exercising their giftedness.

Giftedness is power. Yes, humans have significant limitations. None of us is omnicompetent, and even all of us put together are not omnipotent.[8] But the energy that God has placed into any one of us is amazing. The energy available when we combine our gifts and work together is incalculable.

That's why you need to find out what your giftedness is and exercise it with authority.

WHAT MAKES WORK "SIGNIFICANT"?

I've worked with lots of people who are eager to discover their "workmanship" so they can go do the "good works" that God has in mind for them. But a common assumption is that "good works" are to be found in vocational "ministry" (i.e., church work), or else in the social sector (nonprofits, education, the so-called helping professions). Everyday work is, well, less important, less noble. It's just about making money.

That mentality has been around for a long time. Usually it's ascribed to the fifth century BC and the Greek philosopher Plato. Whenever it began, people at some point started dividing the world into "higher" and "lower" categories. That dualism permeated Western thought, and people sorted occupations into more important work and less important work. In Christianity, it led to the notion of "sacred" work—the work of priests, nuns, ministers, missionaries—and "secular" work, meaning all other kinds of work. Along with that came a distinction between the "clergy" and the "laity."

This philosophical hangover is especially bedeviling to knowledge workers, who tend to seek meaning in their work, want to make a difference with their lives, and have options for what kinds of jobs they can choose. Yet they have thousands of years of popular thought and church tradition telling them that the only work that matters is "God's work."

But God has never divided human work into more important work and less important work. He just gives us the gift of work[9] and fits each of us with a particular giftedness to do a particular kind of work.[10] So if someone says certain work is more important than other kinds of work, they are implying that certain kinds of giftedness (and therefore people) are more important than other kinds of giftedness (and therefore people). That will never wash.

This sacred-secular dichotomy, as it is often called, is nothing but a snare that will prevent you from ever seeing your work as something God cares about. And if God doesn't care about your work, then how can He care about you, given that work—whether it's paid work or not[11]—is where you spend the bulk of your time and energy?

No wonder countless people muddle through life with the vague sense that God only cares about their eternal destiny but has nothing to say about their work. God ends up having no part in that huge area of their life, because He's irrelevant to it. Or so they assume.[12]

As a result, work so easily becomes corrupted and nothing like the blessing that God intended for us (more on that in a moment). But how can a gift from God not become corrupted if God is left out of it?

And then there's the whole mindset that says social sector work (non-profit organizations, education, health care, philanthropy, etc.) is somehow inherently more significant than other kinds of employment. An extreme of this distinction is to hold up Mother Teresa on the one hand, and greedy Wall Street types on the other. Charity is good; business is bad. Sure, we may have to go make a buck when we're younger and raising a family, but at some point we should let go of that nasty, dirty business world and "give back." We should do something "significant."

But as we've seen, *all* work has value and significance, because people themselves have value and significance. Do I think it's more significant for someone to work with an autistic child than to mow a lawn? I can see why most people would say that it is. Certainly those two jobs differ in complexity and consequences. But I'm not God, so I'm not really in a position to rank the significance of one over the other. I love the fact that someone is gifted to the task of helping the child. But if I'm that child's father, mowing lawns may be the only way I have to pay for that care. Is my work any less significant?

We'll talk more in chapter 7 about how you might determine where to best deploy your gifts. For now keep in mind that "nonprofit" is just a tax status. There's nothing *inherently* significant about nonprofit work. If you think there is, then you're conferring divine authority on the Internal Revenue Service to be the arbiter of what is and is not "significant"!

Perhaps the real source of misunderstanding about this significance thing is that we've got the significance of everyday, for-profit work all screwed up. We place huge value (as in monetary value) on things that really don't amount to much, and grossly undervalue (i.e., underpay) stuff that makes all the difference in the world for how people actually live and what we are leaving behind for future generations.

I don't have the answer to all of that, but I know one thing: significance is not about where you work or what you do for work but about what's driving your work and how you do whatever work you do.

WORK AS A CURSE

No matter how noble a vision for work Genesis 1 may offer, it's no secret that most people today regard their work as more of a curse than a blessing. At best, it's a necessary evil. So what difference does it make that work was intended for good if for most it's turned out to be so bad?

Well, we're back to where we were in the last chapter, talking about the "bad truth" again. That bad truth is that whatever we humans touch, we have a way of making a mess of it. Nowhere do we see that more than in work. We've turned work into drudgery for many—in fact, into outright slavery for too many.

Just consider the many ways in which people have corrupted work—through injustice, deception, fraud, bribery, nepotism, favoritism, greed, envy, arrogance, laziness, workaholism, lust, gossip, slander, cheating, rumormongering, recklessness, carelessness, incompetence, waste, prejudice and racism, threats, bullying, violence, murder, genocide, on and on. No wonder so many people hate their jobs!

> What good is your giftedness in a world gone so horribly wrong?

And those are just the ones who have jobs. As of 2012, an estimated 197 million people worldwide were without jobs, and another 39 million had dropped out of the labor market.[13] Those numbers don't count the 1.1 billion people who currently subsist below the internationally accepted "extreme-poverty" threshold of $1.25 US per day.[14]

The unemployed and the extremely poor remind us that work is indeed a blessing and a gift. Perhaps you've heard the platitude that "no one

ever comes to the end of their life and says, 'I wish I had worked more.'"
Whoever came up with that obviously was never unemployed.

IS GIFTEDNESS JUST A LUXURY?

So what good is your giftedness in a world gone so horribly wrong? I
get asked that question a lot, especially by people living in circumstances
that offer no real options for where they might "choose" to work.

Is giftedness just a luxury?

The answer is unequivocally no. Giftedness is not a luxury, it's a reality. It's part of being human. The peasant in the rice paddy in North
Korea has their own unique giftedness every bit as much as the knowledge worker at the trendy fast company in Silicon Valley. If people have
options—and one definition of affluence is that you have options—those
options don't increase people's giftedness, they only increase the possibilities for where and how people might be able to express their giftedness and use it to provide for their needs.

That's why the men who founded the United States were so passionately devoted to the value of freedom. They instinctively perceived that
each individual has their own particular way of wanting to engage the
world—what the Declaration of Independence describes as "the pursuit
of happiness." They wanted freedom—options—to allow each man[15] to
follow that pursuit as he saw fit.

It's worth observing that the final draft of the Declaration specifically
names the pursuit of happiness as an "unalienable Right" endowed upon
humankind by "their Creator." It is indeed! That's why I believe every human in the world deserves freedom, because wherever people have had
it, they've benefitted in every way—materially, economically, socially,
personally, and spiritually.[16]

However, this book is not about solving global poverty or advocating
for human rights. It's about you. I want to help you make your life count
for something. You instinctively feel that you were put here for a purpose. That's because you were, as we've seen.

So how do you figure out what your "workmanship," or giftedness,
is and then link it up with meaningful work that pays you enough to express it? We'll explore those questions in parts II and III.

PART II

SO HOW DO YOU FIND YOUR GIFTEDNESS?

THE TRUTH HIDDEN IN PLAIN SIGHT

Have you ever lost something and then found it right under your nose? You end up feeling kind of sheepish. But some things just have a way of eluding your notice.

One time I was flying home with a carry-on bag plus a black, leather portfolio containing some work-related material and my iPad. The procedure at the airport was to show your ID to a couple of security personnel and then board a tram to your terminal. There you would go through the full security check. So I presented my license, boarded the transport, arrived at my terminal, went through security, and retrieved my belongings. It was then that I realized: Where's my portfolio?

Mentally I backtracked my steps as I raced back to the tram and returned to the main terminal. I headed over to the ticket counter where I had obtained my boarding pass at a kiosk. No one there knew anything about a black, leather portfolio. I called the people who had taken me to the airport, thinking maybe I had left it in their car. They checked the vehicle and found nothing. Exasperated, I used the Find My iPad app on my iPhone. It showed that my device was still at the airport. That was good. At least no one had run off with it—yet. Perhaps someone had turned it in to Lost and Found, located at the airport police department. I went there. Nothing.

With time running out, I needed to go back to my terminal and get to my gate. So with a sick feeling, I returned to the security stand at the departure for the tram. As I walked up to the two guards working there, my eyes popped out of my head! Sitting on the podium right in front of the two TSA officers was my portfolio—apparently unnoticed and untouched from when I had laid it there earlier to grab my wallet and present my ID.

I walked up to the station, presented my license, waited for clearance, thanked the officer, put my wallet back in my pocket, picked up my portfolio, and boarded the tram. The security personnel were none the wiser. I had retrieved my portfolio—and its valuable contents—and went on my way without incident.

Sometimes a thing can be hidden in plain sight.

WHY IT'S SO HARD TO SEE YOUR OWN GIFTEDNESS

You would think that since your giftedness is so dominant in your life, you would instinctively know what it is. But not so. I don't think any of us on our own fully recognizes our own giftedness.

The reason is that you live inside your skin. It's the same reason for why you can't see your own face. You can see every other face in the world, but it's a physical impossibility to see your own face. You can see it if you look in a mirror, but even then you only see a reflection. I suppose the only way to see your face as others see it is to have an "out-of-body" experience by looking at a photo of it or watching a video of it.

The same is true for your giftedness. You can see other people's giftedness. But it's almost impossible to see your own giftedness because when you're using it, you're not thinking about using it—you're just using it. It's natural. It's instinctive. It doesn't seem remarkable. You wouldn't think of doing life any other way. As a result, your giftedness proves a bit elusive.

That's important to remember the next time you try to help someone else (like your twentysomething son or a friend who hates her job) think about what they should do with their life. It does no good to ask them, "What are you good at?" or, "What would you like to do?" They honestly may not know. It's not because they're not bright or they lack insight. It's because they live inside their skin, and although they have the subjective experience of using their giftedness, they can't articulate exactly what it is.

Giftedness is a truth hidden in plain sight—as plain as the nose on your face, actually. But then, you can't see your nose, can you?

THE ASSESSMENT INDUSTRY

That's why we now have a whole industry devoted to what is called "assessment."

With the rise of knowledge work in the mid-twentieth century, it became apparent that different people add value differently. In knowledge work, you can't just change out people the way you change parts in an engine. One person excels at analyzing numbers, but the next person doesn't. One person is great at building a relationship and making a sale, but someone else is not. So how do you know who should do what?

Industry turned to the military for the answer to that question. Since World War I, the military had been using IQ tests and the like to sort and slot recruits. The military had won World War II, so obviously they must have known what they were doing, right?

Is taking a test the best way to find out your giftedness?

Thus the door opened for the wide-scale use of "psychometric" tools in the workplace, and a whole new industry was born. Today there are hundreds, possibly thousands, of personality inventories, psychological profiles, preference questionnaires, and other assessments on the market. Just a few of the more well known include: Myers-Briggs, DISC, StrengthsFinder, Caliper, Johnson-O'Connor, AIMS, Strong-Campbell, Birkman, Predictive Index, Wechsler Adult Intelligence Scale, MMPI, the Enneagram, Lion/Otter/Beaver/Retriever, True Colors. Many NFL teams use the Wonderlic test to assess the smarts of aspiring quarterbacks. Other fields likewise have preferred assessments to fit their own particular needs.

So is taking a test the best way to find out what your giftedness is? Well, consider the widely popular Myers-Briggs Type Indicator (MBTI). It sorts people into sixteen different "types," or preferred ways of perceiving the world and making decisions. Once you discover your type, you have all kinds of insight into yourself. Sounds pretty good. You now know what makes you different from people in the fifteen other type categories. But what distinguishes you from the people in your own type?

For example, let's say you're an ESTJ (Extroverted-Sensing-Thinking-Judging). ESTJs comprise an estimated 8.7 percent of the population of the United States.[1] That's 27.3 million people. Extrapolated to the entire world, that's 613 million people. I've stressed again and again that your giftedness is unique to you. So if tens and even hundreds of millions of other people are the same "type" as you, does figuring out what your type is nail down what your giftedness is? I think not.

Look, I have nothing against Myers-Briggs. I've occasionally worked with it myself, and I think it offers some interesting insights into human interactions. I just don't see it getting down to the individual, personal level, which is where the giftedness lies.

The same could be said for nearly all other assessment approaches. They describe people in terms of categories, or tendencies, or placement on a scale, or deviation from a statistical "norm." All of that is inherently comparative. But what we need to know is not how you compare *to* other people; rather, we need to learn what distinguishes you *from* other people. What makes you uniquely you?

GETTING TO THE HEART OF THE MATTER

I believe that all assessments are looking at the phenomenon of giftedness, whether the test's designers realize it or not. They are trying to describe a human being. But that turns out to be an exceedingly difficult task. Not only are people complex, but you have to figure out what is relevant to even look for, let alone how to look for and how to describe it.

Think of it this way. Suppose the renowned cellist Yo-Yo Ma agreed to submit to a psychophysiological study on what happens when he is in the sweet spot playing his instrument. So he takes a battery of psychological profiles and personality tests. Then he is hooked up to no end of electrodes, probes, wires, and devices that can measure his pulse, heart rate, oxygen levels, brain wave activity, galvanic skin responses, muscle movements, eye focus, metabolism, and scores of other data on what is going on with him.

Once all the equipment is in place, Ma begins to play. He's allowed to warm up and get "into" the music—into what psychologists call his "flow" state.[2] All of the readouts from the technology get sampled and recorded. Later, the researchers compile a summary of what was going on when Ma seemed lost in the hauntingly contemplative Sarabande movement of Bach's *Suite No. 5 in C minor*. They've got reams of data and scores of reports. It's all terribly interesting, and it's all accurate.

There's just one problem: none of it tells us why Yo-Yo Ma gets out of bed in the morning to play his cello. To discover that, we need a different approach.

THE SUBJECTIVITY OF ASSESSMENT

How did people figure out what their giftedness was a thousand or two thousand years ago (not that anyone needed to think much about giftedness at that time)? They did it by getting feedback from others around them.

Over time, for example, the people in a village might notice that one particular farmer just always seemed to get a greater yield from his crops than everyone else. Other individuals were known for being exceptionally good at taming horses, or doing beadwork, or shooting an arrow, or shaping wood. Meanwhile, one woman would gain a reputation as an incredible cook, another for weaving, another for singing, another for match-making. People instinctively saw various strengths and abilities in others and commented on them.

> The perceptions of others aren't a very reliable way to understand your giftedness.

That's really no different than what you probably experienced in grade school. At recess, everyone knew which kids they wanted on their softball team. Certain kids were better at the game, and others made great team players. Then after recess, the teacher announced a team spelling contest. Everyone immediately knew whose team they wanted to be on. They had learned by experience that some kids were better with words than others.

This process of learning about ourselves from others is how we all gain some rudimentary awareness of our giftedness. From our earliest days we receive feedback—whether verbal or nonverbal—from our parents, from our parents' acquaintances, from our siblings and their acquaintances, from teachers, coaches, peers, and so on. Other people have a way of telling us what they see. That process has a powerful way of shaping our self-image.

It is also highly and inherently subjective. Other people form and express their *perceptions* of us, based on what they see. But they can't see what's inside of us. So even if their perception is somewhat accurate, it always lacks the full context of what's going on inside us. This is such an important point that we'll come back to it when we talk about relationships in chapter 8.

Getting feedback from others can be helpful but also harmful (90 percent of the people who come my way have been shamed for the very thing that is their real giftedness; again, more on that later). The perceptions of others aren't a very reliable way to understand your giftedness.

Psychometric tools try to get around that subjectivity by scientifically measuring aspects of a person. The designers identify certain characteristics or "traits" that they want to quantify. They then create questions aimed at pinpointing what those traits are for you.

For example, a test might ask you a series of forced-choice questions along the lines of:

When learning a new task, which of the following approaches do you most prefer?
A. Reading a book.
B. Listening to an expert.
C. Watching someone demonstrate it.
D. Experimenting with it on your own.

A computer then tallies your responses and your scores are compared to a "norm" of the population. It then generates a report that purports to describe you.

Many assessment reports look very impressive. They include graphs and charts and scores and percentiles. They may even integrate your scores into narrative paragraphs that describe how you tend to behave or feel. All in all, they come across as very scientific, analytical, and objective.

But the objectivity of a test is not determined by how it reports its findings, or even whether a computer algorithm was involved in the process. It all depends on where the information comes from in the first place.

Where does it come from? It comes from you. When you answer an inventory question, you are *self-appraising*. You are telling the testing people whatever you end up telling them—based on your own self-insight (or lack thereof) gained through a lifetime of experiences, including the subjective perceptions of others. The assumption is that you know yourself well enough to accurately answer the question. But what if you don't?

And what if you fudge on an answer? What if you check an answer that you know isn't really you? After all, you may have reasons for wanting the test to come out a certain way (e.g., to get a job, to get accepted into a program, to come across a certain way to potential love interests). For that reason, some test designers put questions in their tests to assess how "truthful" someone is being. But to me that's an admission of an essential flaw in psychometrics: they are inherently subjective, because their data is based on self-reporting.

Again, I don't want to dismiss psychometrics out of hand. They have their use. They tend to be fast, inexpensive, and scalable—just what industry likes. But in the current state of the art, their ability to assess people's giftedness is about as good as a backyard telescope's ability to see the stars. They get us in the ballpark, which is helpful. But they don't tell us how *you* uniquely play your position.

THE POWER OF STORY

There is, however, a categorically different way of understanding you. Remember that giftedness manifests itself as a pattern of motivation and behavior in your life. That pattern starts expressing itself very early, and you repeat that same basic pattern again and again.

So what if you go back in your life and revisit some of those moments when you were living out that pattern? If what I'm saying is true, you should be able to gather evidence from those moments that brings to light whatever your motivational pattern, or giftedness, happens to be.

In other words, you should be able to discover your giftedness from your own life story.

Now as soon as I talk about "story," some people will immediately object. "Stories? Bill, you were just complaining about personality tests being subjective. What could possibly be more subjective than stories?" (People who ask that obviously haven't spent much time in the humanities.)

I grant that a lot of stories in our world are pure fiction. Writers like Stephen King, John Grisham, and Mary Higgins Clark have made fortunes concocting gripping but totally imaginative tales of love, murder, international espionage, and all manner of other themes.

But other stories are totally objective in that they actually happened in the real world. The Invasion of Normandy was no fiction. Neither was the building of the Golden Gate Bridge. Nor was the game between the Texas Rangers and the Toronto Blue Jays on May 1, 1991 when Nolan Ryan pitched the seventh no-hitter of his career, setting an MLB record that still stands.

In your life, at certain moments, certain activities have captured your interest in some compelling way. You may have lost yourself in that activity. You got completely involved in it. You accomplished something—maybe not anything particularly impressive to others but nonetheless something important to you. You recall that activity as energizing and satisfying. In fact, you might not mind doing it again.

Can you think of such an activity right now?

Maybe it was the time when you were seven, and you and your brother built a tree house in the backyard. You spent hours working on that project, and you loved it. Once it was built, you spent hours up there in a special club with your friends.

Or maybe it was history class in middle school. You didn't even like history. But there was this one assignment about a battle in fifteenth-century England. For whatever reason, you really got into that project. You went to the school library and checked out books and read encyclopedias on it. You drew maps. You had to give a report on what you'd learned, so you dressed up like a knight and made a presentation before the class. When you were done, you got a standing ovation, and the teacher gave you one of only two As that she handed out for that assignment. It was the highlight of seventh grade!

Or maybe it was the trip to Africa when you visited an orphanage. You took your video camera along and recorded lots of scenes from your travels. When you got back, you decided to edit that footage into a video that told the stories of the orphans. You posted the video on YouTube, and next thing you know, 380,000 people had viewed it. The orphanage started receiving inquiries about how people could donate, and a few wanted to know how they could adopt some of the children.

Maybe you can remember a scene from your childhood, or maybe it's something that happened as recently as last week. When it took place isn't what matters. What matters is that it was a moment in your life that met two criteria: (a) you were actually doing something (as opposed to just passively experiencing something, like watching a TV show or visiting the mountains in Colorado), and (b) you took satisfaction from the activity. You enjoyed doing it. You gained energy from doing it.

The satisfaction is the key. The telltale sign that your giftedness is engaged in an activity is that you take joy or satisfaction in doing it.

You can find some other examples of satisfying activities on page 207 in the section in the back entitled "Discovering Your Giftedness: A Step-by-Step Guide."

SEEING THE WORLD THROUGH YOUR EYES

The satisfying activities of your life hold incredibly valuable clues as to what your giftedness is all about. And those stories are actually the most objective way to discover it. Because they actually happened in the real world. You're not making them up. You're not talking about what you might do in a hypothetical situation, or what you think you might be like, or any other form of self-appraisal. No, you're talking about what you actually did. If we had a video of you while you were doing those activities, we would actually see you doing the things you're reporting about.

Yes, you would tell the stories from your "point of view." To that extent, your reports are subjective. But that's exactly what we would want! If we're going to discover *your* giftedness, we have to look at the world through your eyes. We have to see what matters to *you*, what *you* pay attention to, what *you* find satisfying, and how *you* do life.

Your stories turn out to be the ideal way to do that. As a result, they capture the essence of you.

It's a lot like studying an athlete using game film. Suppose we wanted to know how Phil Mickelson swings a golf club. We could watch a bunch of video of him swinging a golf club—especially when he hits the ball in the "sweet spot" of the club and puts it right on the green, one short putt away from the cup. By analyzing lots of film on how he does that, we would see all kinds of idiosyncrasies in his particular swing. We could see how his swing differs from other people's swing, but more importantly we would get down to the individual level: How does Phil Mickelson uniquely swing a club?

By analyzing what you are actually doing when you're in the "sweet spot" of your giftedness, we can accurately describe what that giftedness is. It's revealed out of your own life story.

In "Discovering Your Giftedness: A Step-by-Step Guide," I've given you a method for telling stories about your satisfying activities and then analyzing those stories to find your particular pattern of giftedness. If you're using this book to help you decide what direction to go with your life, I'd encourage you to pause and go through that exercise before reading the next chapter and part III. The material that follows will make a lot more sense and be a lot more useful to you once you've gained that insight into your giftedness.

TELL YOUR STORIES, DON'T JUST REMEMBER THEM

Before sending you off on that task, however, I want to point out why telling stories is such a powerful means of accessing your core personhood—infinitely better than taking a test. It's because you're a person, and one of the essential needs of any person is to be known, to be seen, to be heard. Humans who are never known, seen, or heard are scarcely humans at all.

That's why I insist that unless you're dealing with some rather unusual circumstances, you really should go through the exercise in the back of the book with someone else. Just think about it: you're going to be recalling some of the best moments of your life, the times when, for whatever reason, the planets lined up and you were doing the thing you were born to do. There is something powerfully affirming about *telling* another person the stories of those moments.

And then to have that other person be there as you wake up to the amazing "good truth" that is inside you—well, for many people, it's simply overwhelming! I've never seen anyone break into tears upon receiving the results of their Myers-Briggs test or DISC profile. But I've seen many people moved to tears when it finally dawns on them what it is they've been trying to express their whole life. I'm not saying everyone has that reaction, and there's nothing wrong with you if you don't. But with or without any strong emotions, having another person understand and confirm your giftedness is nothing short of transformative.

WARNING:

IDENTIFYING YOUR GIFTEDNESS IS NOT ENOUGH

God was standing in the nursery of heaven, creating three human beings—two men and a woman. To the first man He said, "You shall be named William Wilberforce, and you shall bring an end to slavery in England!"

Wilberforce replied, "Thy will be done, Lord."

To the woman God said, "You shall be called Mother Teresa, and you shall bring dignity to the least of the least in Calcutta."

Mother Teresa replied, "Thy will be done, Lord."

Finally, to the other man God said, "You shall be called Donald Trump, and you shall wash cars in Brooklyn."

To which Donald Trump replied, "You're fired!"

FAIL FACTORS

To be fair to the Donald, I suspect he's ended up right where he was designed to end up—doing deals and getting himself noticed. He sure appears to be in the sweet spot.

You may not be so fortunate.

My premise in this book is that you arrive in the world with a particular bent, or giftedness, which fits you for a particular function. If you figure out what your giftedness is, it will tell you what you should do with your life. Then you can go do that.

I totally buy that premise. But when I look at the actual experience of people, I run into an inconvenient truth: just because someone knows their giftedness doesn't mean they end up acting on it. I could fill a book with stories of people who have gone through no end of assessments to identify their strengths, motivations, talents, intelligence, aptitudes, interests, preferences, passions, personality type, leadership style, sales quotient, conflict pattern, and other characteristics. Yet after all of that, they're still at square one.

They're like a rocket on a launching pad, all fueled up, all ready to go, coordinates locked in, all systems go—but then at the final moment, the mission gets scrubbed. There's a failure to launch.

In popular language we call that an "epic fail," a complete and total breakdown that confounds what we would have expected.

What accounts for epic fails in terms of life and career direction? How do people stall out and get stuck in a holding pattern instead of venturing out to embrace the "good works" that have been prepared for them?

Years ago I started a list of reasons to account for that. I keep adding to it all the time. In this chapter I want to mention just a few of those reasons—not to scare you but to caution you that discovering your giftedness is not enough in itself to get you where you need to go.

Unfortunately, I don't have space to discuss all of these challenges in detail, much less to give you in-depth answers for overcoming them. But if I can help you put a name on what holds you back, you can at least start owning that limiting factor. That's the first step in dealing with it.

In truth, there are so many reasons why people stall out that I've clustered them into eight families of "epic fail factors," as follows:

I'm not saying these are the only factors. But if you're stuck, if you're having a hard time "getting going," or "figuring it out," or "getting your act together," or "doing something," or whatever you want to call it, you've got some sort of "fail factor" holding you back (you may have more than one; many of them are interrelated). Let's see which family yours might belong to.

FAIL FACTOR #1: IGNORANCE

I'm talking about the ignorance of not having a clear understanding of your giftedness. I can't say that not knowing your giftedness makes it impossible to do the thing you were put here to do, any more than I can say that knowing your giftedness automatically leads to doing the thing you were put here to do. Plenty of people do spectacular things even though they have no clue what their giftedness is. How fortunate for them!

Let me just state categorically that *most people don't know what their giftedness is, except at a very rudimentary level.* Even in the United States, where it's become popular to affirm people's uniqueness, most people still have at best a superficial understanding of their core strengths and motivation.

"Well, I think I know myself pretty well." I hear that all the time (especially from men; they don't always say it, but they think it so loudly I can hear it). "I think I know myself pretty well. I don't need no stinkin' personality test to tell me about myself!"

Maybe. But more than likely not.

The more successful you are, the greater the temptation to think you've got yourself figured out. My experience shows otherwise. That's because I get called in on the epic fails, the cases where someone who is brilliant and has succeeded in everything they ever put their mind to has nevertheless inexplicably crashed and burned. They and everyone else are mystified and racking their brains, wondering, "What happened?!" In almost every case, we discover that one of the key contributing factors was simple ignorance of how the person is fundamentally wired to function.

So how do you know whether you have a good enough understanding of your giftedness? Here's an exercise to find out:

HOW WELL DO YOU KNOW YOURSELF?

The best indicator of how well you know your giftedness is that you can use it to predict ahead of time what will happen if you place yourself in a given set of circumstances.

Instructions: For each question below, rate how well you think you can answer that question, using the following scale:

1	2	3	4	5
DON'T KNOW	MIGHT KNOW BUT NOT SURE	KIND OF KNOW	THINK I KNOW PRETTY WELL	KNOW EXACTLY

SCORE

If you take a certain job, given the realities of that job, do you know where you're going to thrive and where you're just going to survive?

If you're placed on a team, do you know which role would be best for you on that team? Do you know how you instinctively will try to relate to the other people on that team? Can you predict whom you will most easily clash with, based on how you're wired?

Do you know who you need around you to be most effective (i.e., what kinds of giftedness you need to complement yours)? Do you know whom you can be most useful to (i.e., what kinds of giftedness yours can best complement)?

Do you know how long you're liable to stay motivated on a given assignment? Will you know the signals that your interest and motivation for it are starting to wane?

Would you know whether an assignment or role definitely does not have your name on it?

Do you know what kind of supervision or management is ideal for you?

Do you know how you would oversee other people? Do you know whether you have any motivation to oversee other people?

Do you know the ideal working conditions for you to do your best stuff?

Do you know how you prefer to communicate to other people? Do you know whether you even prefer to communicate to other people?

Do you know how you try to influence other people? Do you know whether you even care to influence other people?

Do you know what the "content" of your job should be? Should you work with numbers? Money? Groups of people? Individuals? Experts? Concepts? Transactions? Problems? Needs? Crises? Learners? Animals?

Do you know what drives your behavior, the motivational "payoff" that you instinctively seek? Is it really to "make money"? Or is it to meet a challenge? Or meet a need? Or come out on top? Or take down the bad guys? Or gain understanding? Or make a difference? Or be heard? Or get a deal done? Or conceivably make money grow? Or what?

TOTAL SCORE

SCORE

54–60 Congratulations! You appear to have an excellent understanding of your giftedness.

44–53 You know your giftedness reasonably well, but need some clarification.

31–43 You have a bit of insight into your giftedness, but not enough to make key decisions.

12–30 You have no real understanding of your giftedness and are at significant risk as a result.

If you think this survey is asking unfair questions, think again. It merely asks questions that life asks people every day, whether they realize it or not. The reason so many come up short on answering them is because they don't know themselves very well. They don't know their giftedness.

Remember, your giftedness is a domino against which all the other dominoes in your life are leaning. So if that key domino keeps falling down—because you don't know what it is, or you're misguided about it, or you have a superficial understanding of it, or you're missing key pieces of it—then those other dominoes will keep falling down, as well.

FAIL FACTOR #2: FEAR

Countless people who know something about their giftedness remain stuck because they are terrified of making a mistake. (This is not the same as the person who doesn't want to make a mistake, which is why they seek to discover how they're intrinsically wired.)

Usually that fear gets expressed through an imagined "what-if" scenario: "What if it doesn't work?" "What if I get out there and fall on my face?" "What if I launch off in this new direction and find out I don't really have what it takes (i.e., I'm not talented/smart/creative/tough/clever enough, or whatever)?" "What if I can't make a living doing this?"

When I was a freshman in college, I was assigned to a graduate student as my advisor for picking courses. He was in his thirties. He already had two master's degrees, now he was pursuing a third! I suspect that fellow not only didn't know what his giftedness was but was afraid of committing to a career, with the result that he had turned into a professional student. Imagine: he was advising me on what direction *I* should go!

> If I'm trapped in a burning building, I don't want the fireman standing around fretting, "But what if I don't succeed?"

If you examine your fear, you'll probably find a fear beneath the fear. So for instance: "What if I fall on my face?" Well, what if you did? What would that look like? What would happen? "Oh, my world would fall apart," you might say. But again, what does that mean?

It can mean different things to different people, but one of the most common "fears beneath the fear" is worrying what other people will think—especially family and friends. It's really a form of stage fright, of worrying that you'll embarrass yourself.

But notice something about that particular fear: it's excessively self-focused. You're worried about what *you* will look like, how *you* might embarrass *yourself*, how *your* reputation might be affected. It's not a focus on the gift, much less on an opportunity where it might be expressed.

So if what you're really fearing is the possibility of a tarnished image, I want to point out that giftedness works best when you're not focused on yourself but on the situation at hand that needs your giftedness. If I'm trapped in a burning building, I don't want the fireman standing around fretting, "But what if I don't succeed? What if I'm not strong/fast/smart enough? What will people think if I fall on my face?" No, I want him to see the flames and smell the smoke and hear me shouting for help, because all those cues will trigger his motivation for confronting danger and keeping a cool head in a crisis, and he'll instinctively kick down the door and come find me.

I could craft a similar analogy for your gift. The point is, fear is inherently self-absorbing. So one of the best, fastest ways to surmount it is to refocus on a situation that could use what you are wired to do. If you're truly gifted to that task, your motivational juices will start flowing, and you'll be drawn toward taking action.

But of course, the path of least resistance for someone who is afraid is to play it safe. Sadly, that's what a majority of young adults end up doing. Instead of trusting that their innate gifts have actual power—including the power to earn a living—they choose the safety and (seeming) security of the best-paying job they can find. Basically they treat their giftedness like it's a hobby instead of a reality, something to only indulge on weekends.

Some of them play the game of thinking, "Let me go make a bunch of money first and get squared away financially. Then I can afford to get back to this giftedness thing."

Either way, it's a devil's bargain. Because the person who plays it safe is almost always overlooking the potential upside of not playing it safe—in other words, the opportunity cost. Yes, there's always the possibility that trying to follow your giftedness won't "work." But what if it did work? And what would you be missing out on if it did? Perhaps more importantly, what might the world be missing out on if you ignore your giftedness and "play it safe"?

Fear drives you to think of worst-case scenarios. But when it comes to giftedness, worst-case scenarios are never the result of using your giftedness but of not using it. Earlier I mentioned Nik Wallenda, the tightrope walker. I wouldn't dream of walking across the Grand Canyon, because I don't have the giftedness to do that. But Nik Wallenda does. So while, yes, he could imagine any number of terrible things happening, his giftedness is actually what enables him to confront those scenarios and figure out how to avoid them. The only true "worst-case" scenario for Nik Wallenda would be to *not* walk across the Grand Canyon. He couldn't live with himself if he didn't do that!

What does your giftedness tell you about what you can't live without doing? Were you born to solve problems? Then you can't truly live without solving problems. Were you born to cause learning to take place? Then you won't be able to live with yourself unless you're causing others to learn. Were you born to tell stories? Your soul won't survive unless you tell stories.

Look around you. It's not the people who have played it safe who are the most alive. It's the people who, for whatever reason, grab hold of their giftedness and trust it to see them through. Does it feel risky for them to do that? You bet! But where's the gain if you have nothing to lose? That's why my father used to warn his students, "My fear is not that you would fail but that you will succeed in doing the wrong thing."

FAIL FACTOR #3: DOUBT

Doubt is the conjoined twin of fear. Your giftedness resides in your personhood, so self-doubt is really the fear that you don't have what it takes.

I suppose the most common way people express doubt about their gift is to say, "No one will ever pay me to do that." I hear that all the time.

I worked with a doctor once (he also had an MBA) who had the most marvelous gift for helping experts with specialized knowledge understand one another. When I showed him that, he nodded in agreement, then looked at me with a blank stare. "Yeah, I can see that," he affirmed, "but what good is it?" I about fell off my chair!

What good is it? Are you kidding me? Here we live in a world of knowledge workers whose niches of proficiency grow more sophisticated, but also more isolated, by the day. It's like a modern-day Tower of Babel, with everyone speaking a different language. How valuable is the person who can speak all of those languages and translate them for everyone else?

Whenever someone says to me, "No one will ever pay me to do what I'm gifted to do," I ask them a simple question: Is *anyone* getting paid to do what you're gifted to do? If the answer is yes, then that falsifies their assertion. Someone is, in fact, getting paid to do that. So now the question becomes: How can you become one of those people?

For example, imagine someone whose gift boils down to talking with people and commenting on what they're hearing. How could anyone possibly make a living using such a talent? Well, according to *Forbes*, Oprah Winfrey has made about $2.9 billion doing exactly that.[1]

How are you going to get paid to do what God has designed you to do? I don't know! That's a marketing question you have to figure out. And you're going to have to think and explore and be creative and resourceful to figure it out. But the worst thing you can do is abandon your gift and settle just because the answer to that question doesn't seem obvious.

I can't guarantee that you'll be able to make a living in this world, with or without your giftedness. But I know one thing: people who are among the best in the world at what they do have an infinitely better shot of getting hired over people who are mere pretenders.

FAIL FACTOR #4: PRESSURE

One time an accountant came to see me because he was totally burned out in his job. So we worked together to assess his gifts and then met to discuss the results. I began the feedback session by joking, "Steve, the stage lost a great talent the day you decided to go into accounting."

To my surprise, the man teared up. "I'm sorry," I immediately responded.

"No, no," he said, holding up his hand with a faint smile. "You didn't do anything wrong. The truth is, when I was in college I was going to major in drama. But my dad was a banker, so he was totally against that. 'Son,' he told me, 'that's completely impractical. You'll never make a living in the theater.' I had taken a test that said I was good with numbers, so Dad said I should go into accounting. 'You can always find a job in accounting,' he told me. So that's what I did. And here I am.'"

I've probably encountered hundreds of people like that man, who have succumbed to the pressure of parental expectations. Somewhere inside them a voice (their giftedness) is telling them what they ought to do, but that voice gets drowned out by the more authoritative voice of their parents.

Please understand, most parents only want the best for their children. They're offering the most sound advice they know how to give when they steer them away from one path and toward another. Their intentions are good. But somehow their child's giftedness doesn't get factored into their thinking.

And it's not just the expectations of your parents that can put pressure on you. The culture you've grown up in, along with the values and assumptions of the larger society, can heavily affect your choices.

Probably the most naturally gifted person I've ever seen in terms of raw administrative and managerial horsepower was a woman who had grown up in extreme poverty. No one ever told her to think about college. At most they might have encouraged her to learn some computer skills and become an admin at a business or law firm. Somehow she managed to attend junior college. But I can only imagine how far she might have gone had she grown up under different expectations and advantages.

If parents and society can put pressure on you to lean away from honoring your true bent, your spouse can tighten the screws even more. They also have a vision for their life based on their background of cultural expectations, and you may well factor into those plans.

For example, say your wife's father owns a business. When you and your wife were dating and getting serious, her father was okay about that because at the time you were majoring in business. He was excited about the prospect of a possible business partner and potential successor coming into the family. But then after you got married, you discovered that business was not the best fit for your giftedness. Instead, working with young people—say, as a teacher or counselor or youth worker—would be a better match. That idea may excite you, but what if it wasn't in your wife's plans, let alone her father's plans? Now you've got a challenge on your hands!

FAIL FACTOR #5: TRAPS

The woman who showed up at my office was impeccably dressed and had the most professional demeanor I think I've ever seen. She was in media sales, in what sounded like a fairly impressive job with some nice perks. Nevertheless, she blurted out, "I've got to find a new job, because the one I'm in is killing me!"

Those were strong words, and I felt sad for her. So I asked her, "Why don't you quit?"

"Oh, I have quit," she replied. "I've quit three times."

Needless to say, I was rather perplexed. "Three times? Why do you keep going back?"

> I thought to myself, what a perverse form of slavery to keep working at a job you can't stand just because they pay you lots of money.

"Because every time I quit, they beg me to stay and offer me more money."

I thought to myself, what a perverse form of slavery to keep working at a job you can't stand just because they pay you lots of money. I mean, being able to afford expensive jewelry is nice—but not if it includes a set of golden handcuffs!

I'm not in any way criticizing that woman. She's like so many people in our culture whose giftedness is effectively trapped by the circumstances they choose to stay in.

A more benign version of this fail factor are the many people who say, "I can't stand my job, but I stay there for the health insurance." In fact, I once saw a cartoon of two employees on a coffee break at the office vending machine. One of them says to the other, "My career doesn't reflect what my passions are as much as where my insurance is."

Of course, even as I write, health insurance in the United States is in complete flux, to say the least. So who knows what it will look like in the future? But quite apart from that, working for someone only to collect health insurance seems like a trap to me. It's another form of playing it safe. I suppose if security is what matters most to you, it makes sense. But at what cost?

For lots of young adults nowadays, the trap can be living at home, especially if your parents have made it comfortable to live at home. Listen, I'm thoroughly aware of how bad the job market is for young adults these days. Some 44 percent of recent college graduates in the United States are "underemployed," meaning they have a job, but not one they can live on.[2] So if parents can afford to help their young adult tread water for a while until a decent job comes along, that's great.

But accepting generosity always involves a potential snare. In this case, taking the heat off the question of where you're going to live can easily lower your incentive to find a real job. In other words, Mom and Dad can make it too easy. And so at my practice we've seen plenty of Millennials come through whose parents are only too eager to see their son or daughter figure out their path and get started on it. But the adult child feels no such angst because they've got a sweet deal living at their parents' home, usually rent-free. In a peculiar way they, too, are wearing a set of golden handcuffs.

There are so many traps that keep people from pursuing their giftedness! There's the tyranny of the urgent: the person who is so busy, so committed, so stressed, so rushed that they have no margin to explore the possibilities for a better-fitting situation. Conversely there's the person who is caught in inertia—just kind of drifting along on the river of life, not especially keen on rocking the boat and disrupting the status quo. Their current situation may not be the best, but it would take a lot of time and effort to change things, so change just gets put off.

And then there's the trap of financial debt. When you owe on your house, your car, your credit cards, and your kid's college tuition, to say nothing of your taxes and your monthly expenses, all that matters is staying one step ahead of the hounds. In that case, it's pretty hard not to see giftedness as a luxury. But your giftedness is not a luxury. It's God's gift to you and to the world, intended to bring you great fulfillment and joy. So if you literally can't afford to pursue your gift, then debt is robbing you of your birthright, and you are literally living out the proverb, "The borrower is slave to the lender."[3]

One other trap I must mention has to do with the "dark side" of giftedness (more on that in chapter 9). Your giftedness is intrinsically good, but it has a potential dark side. That is, it can create problems for you and others. Certain kinds of giftedness are inherently susceptible to creating traps for their owners.

For example, let's say you like to get things right. As in, exactly right. That's a perfect gift for doing brain surgery, orthodontics, accounting, surveying, tool and die work, or jewelry repair. But how might that gift affect you if you're exploring better options for work that fits you? It could easily keep you from pursuing a promising possibility because it doesn't look "good enough." You could get trapped in an endless search to find just the "right" job.

Likewise, suppose you're a highly conceptual person who never met an idea you didn't like. That's a delightful gift that could find wonderful expression in so many fields: advertising, journalism, teaching, creative writing, the hospitality industry, museum design, the culinary arts, antiques and collectibles, or publishing, just to name a few. But how might that gift affect you when it comes time to decide on a particular job? One very common tendency is to procrastinate until the opportunity is gone, because saying yes to one option means saying no to so many others.

> How you pursue options that fit your giftedness will itself be driven by your giftedness.

How you pursue options that fit your giftedness will itself be driven by your giftedness, as we'll see in the next chapter.

FAIL FACTOR #6: RESTRICTIONS

In high school, Deke discovered he had a phenomenal arm for throwing a football. His coach was elated. His dad was ecstatic. His girlfriend was impressed. And his mom was—well, just glad he had found a way to pay for college.

But it was all settled. He would sign on with a Division II school where he could showcase his talents. That would draw the attention of a Division I school, and he could move up in his junior year. From there he would have a shot at the NFL. And if that didn't work out, he could still play for the USFL or the Canadian Football League.

That was the plan, anyway. And it started off okay. Following a winning record in the fall of his senior year, Deke was offered a provisional scholarship to a college in Texas. He showed up ready to play. But so did a rival, who won out as the starting quarterback. That sent Deke into a tailspin. But what really took him down was the day he tore his ACL in practice. Bye-bye freshman season.

Deke's spirits sagged. The guys on the team pulled away and he felt totally left out. His girlfriend broke up with him. He started spending his evenings drinking with friends. Before long he was doing drugs, as well. His grades dropped, and by the end of the year, the school sent a letter informing him that his scholarship was being discontinued.

By the time I met Deke, he was trying to get his life back together. He had gotten into rehab and started taking courses at a community college. He wanted to get a new plan for his life. But the booze and drugs had taken their toll, and he was clearly working with a deficit.

I tell you Deke's story because it highlights in rather stark terms what can happen for people who rigidly restrict themselves to following a script for their life and have no alternative plans, or at least flexibility, if that script doesn't come to pass. Planning has its place (as we'll see in a moment). But some people create too much of a plan, and that's almost worse than having no plan at all.

Heavyweight legend Joe Louis is alleged to have said, "Everyone has a plan until they've been hit." That's what people who follow a script fail to consider: the unscripted blow.

In a play or a movie, the script tells all the actors what they're supposed to say and do, and in what sequence, because the story has already been written from beginning to end. But life is not like that. There are definitely actors, but there's no script. Life is more like improvisational theater in which the actors are literally making things up as they go, and a lot of unforeseen elements impinge on what happens.[4]

Nevertheless, you may be trying to control the future. You've predetermined the outcome you want—an outcome that may even take into account your giftedness—and now you're bent on making life cooperate with your plan.

But living that way holds at least two perils. First, it severely restricts your options, because it shuts the door to the unexpected—which includes the unexpected opportunity, not just the unexpected disappointment. Perhaps worse, it predisposes you to resent the unexpected (good or bad) when it does show up. And it will inevitably show up.

I think that accounts for a lot of the negativism and cynicism of our time. A lot of people have had a script for how life was supposed to turn out for themselves and their children. They had a plan and they had no intention of deviating from it. Then they got hit in the face. Now they're bitter because their plan isn't coming together the way they thought it should.

I'm speaking from personal experience here. When I turned forty I was very excited about the decade to come. I had all kinds of hopes, aspirations, and plans. Seven weeks after my birthday, my first wife, Nancy, was diagnosed with breast cancer. That wasn't in my plans. It certainly wasn't in hers. As a family we battled that disease for the next seven years until Nancy died in 2000. Our girls were fifteen, thirteen, and eight, and I was instantly plunged into this thing called single parenting. That wasn't in my plans either. I spent the next ten years getting them ready for life and launching them into the world. Today they're doing great and I'm remarried to Lynn. Needless to say, my life is much, much different from what I expected or planned for it to be.[5]

The interesting thing is that through all of the past fourteen years, life has brought our family many challenges and countless graces, but it's never seemed to care one whit about any of our plans. Life has just rolled on like a mighty river.

And so the takeaway for me is that whatever plans and intentions you or I may have, we always have to write the word "tentative" at the top of that plan, because life gets the final word on what actually happens. As Mark Twain put it, "Don't go around saying the world owes you a living. The world owes you nothing. It was here first."[6]

FAIL FACTOR #7: FOG

As early as 1565, Spanish galleons were traveling between Asia and Cape Mendocino, California, about three hundred miles north of modern-day San Francisco. Laden with goods from China bought with gold from the Americas, the ships traveled along the California coast to Mexico. They stayed well out to sea since dense fog frequently blanketed the coast. As a result, it was not until 1769 that San Francisco Bay was discovered by Europeans—and that occurred only through an expedition on land.

It may be that you're like those Spanish sailors in terms of deploying your giftedness. Innumerable discoveries and opportunities have remained hidden in the fog and passed you by. Worse, you may actually be sailing around in the fog—in which case shipwreck is just a matter of time.

Chief among the "fog failures" is a lack of vision for your life. A vision is not the same as having a goal, although the terms tend to be used interchangeably. Some people are wired to set goals and accomplish them. That's great! But not everyone is like that.[7]

So I prefer the term "vision," because anyone can relate to having a vision. A vision is a picture of where you want to be at some point in the future.

> A vision is like a North Star—always visible, but never attainable.

A vision is like a North Star—always visible, but never attainable. If you have a vision based on your giftedness, it can keep you focused in a clear direction over time, even if you can't predict what will happen day to day.

For example, let's say you have giftedness for exercising ownership and stewardship over things. As a result, you set a goal upon graduating from high school that you're going to own your own business by the time you're twenty-five. You work a plan toward that goal, and then, twenty days before your twenty-fifth birthday, you finalize the ownership agreement on a business you've just purchased. You've reached your goal!

So what is your vision? That's a much bigger matter. It has to do, not with where you'll be in five years but where you want to be in, say, twenty years if you really lean into your giftedness and express it to the full. What might that look like?

Well, to stick with the example above, it would still involve owning and stewarding things. But since you can't know what the world will look like in twenty years, you can't get too specific about what you would own and steward. But you can imagine it! So maybe instead of owning a business you own a string of businesses. Or maybe you no longer own a business, but a piece of property, like a ranch or a resort. Or maybe you don't technically "own" anything, but you nonetheless exercise care over some asset—a school, a church, a community—that you treat as if you actually did own it.

If you have a vision for your life based on your giftedness, you always have a purpose to pursue. You simply use whatever opportunities and resources are at hand to live out that vision in the moment you have.

But what if you have no vision? Then you wander. You flit from thing to thing, job to job, assignment to assignment, relationship to relationship, with no larger, longer-term purpose guiding your choices. In other words, you don't live *intentionally*.

One big reason people end up drifting is because they don't know what their options are. I once worked with a young adult who was a born entertainer. He had played the piano in high school and performed in various productions. He loved Broadway musicals. He had a great sense of humor, especially when he was in his element onstage. But his life was going nowhere. He was toying with the idea of going to business school, even though he had no interest in business. Basically, he was lost.

When I showed him that he had a real gift for engaging an audience of people, he said, "Yeah, I know, but I'm not going to end up on Broadway. I mean, there's no future for people like me."

"Oh yeah?" I shot back. "Have you ever heard of the Experience Economy?"[8] He looked at me blankly and shook his head. "One of the largest segments of our economy any more is based on creating experiences for people," I explained. "The customer doesn't just buy a product or a service; they enter into an experience that engages all of their senses. Think Starbucks, Whole Foods Market, or IMAX theaters.

> High school and college graduates in our culture are aware of only an extremely thin slice of the job possibilities in the work world.

"Within that sector is a whole industry of amusement parks and attractions, museums, historical landmarks, tourist spots, and similar amenities. Ever heard of Williamsburg? The Kilgore Oil Museum in East Texas? Medieval Times? Surely you've heard of Disney World and Six Flags. Places like that employ people like you to entertain audiences."

He had never considered such a thing. And I can understand why. In the main, high school and college graduates in our culture are aware of only an extremely thin slice of the job possibilities in the work world. They (might) understand what their parents do for work, possibly what some of their friends' parents do. And they know what they've seen on TV or in movies. Beyond that, they're clueless. And yet the Occupational Outlook Handbook,[9] which is an online database of occupations kept by the Bureau of Labor Statistics, lists thousands of occupational categories.

Lacking any options to consider, that young man had no way to formulate a vision for where his life could go.

But let's say you did start off with something of a vision—or, failing that, at least some sort of a goal that matters to you. At one point you said, "I want to become an actress." Or, "I aspire to be an expert in a certain period of history." Or, "I want to use my gift for hospitality to run a bed-and-breakfast."

But today, a lot of time has gone by and you're no nearer to accomplishing your objective than you were when you started. Why not? Odds are it's because you're not working a plan to get you from here to your envisioned future. You've got a nice idea that appeals to you, but it's still just an intention. It hasn't translated into action, in real time.

In the previous section I criticized those who overplan their future and try to write a script for what's supposed to happen. You may have the opposite problem: you have no plan. You just have a wish.

A plan is a series of steps aimed at moving you in the direction you want to go. So do you want to become an actress? Great! Did you read any books on acting this past week? Are you staying in the know about what's going on in the theater in your community? Are you initiating any conversations with people in that field? Have you gone online and downloaded any scripts of favorite plays or films and picked out a character and read their lines out loud? Have you worked on memorizing a section of Shakespeare or Anton Chekhov or Andrew Lloyd Webber? Have you auditioned for a part in a community theater production? Have you even just volunteered to do a skit for the junior high kids at your church?

The point is, don't just live with a good intention, even if it's a great fit with your giftedness. *Do* something that takes even one small step toward the realization and actualization of that vision. And then take another. And another. Will you ever arrive at what you envisioned? I can't say. But I can predict with 100 percent accuracy that you'll never arrive at it without working the steps required to get there.

"But I don't know what steps to take!" you say. Well, that's easily solved. In the next chapter I'm going to give you a strategy for getting information about any direction you can conceive of. What you learn through that information-gathering process will tell you most everything you need to know to put a meaningful plan together for accomplishing your vision.

Another factor that may be keeping you in a fog is that you don't have a model to follow. I estimate that somewhere between one-half to two-thirds of all people require someone they can look at and emulate in order to make significant progress in their life. Call that person a mentor, a guide, a coach, a sponsor, a model, or whatever. If you need a person like that and don't have them, you're either going to stay stuck or move a lot more slowly than you would otherwise.

For some people that person is so important I tell them, "You're not looking for a job, you're looking for a person." Indeed, one woman's history of achievement showed a direct correlation between having a modeling individual and not having one. Every single positive development in her life had occurred when she was able to model herself after someone else. Every downward spiral in her life happened when she didn't have that person.

If that sounds anything like you, and you want to get unstuck and on your way to a life that "works," find someone who is doing the thing that you aspire to do and start patterning yourself after them. However . . .

There's just one caveat: beware of pursuing a vision that fits someone else's giftedness but not yours. That's very easy to do. Influential people can have a powerful effect on impressionable minds and imaginations. When John Glenn successfully orbited the earth in 1962, countless American boys decided they wanted to become an astronaut. Obviously only a handful of them actually ended up in that kind of work.

The person whose giftedness is all about relationships will counsel you to focus on building relationships. The person who is all about doing deals will tell you to focus on becoming a savvy negotiator. The person who is all about making an impact will urge you to make an impact with your life, to make a difference (by the way, easily 85 percent of all the senior pastors and teaching pastors I've worked with have had some form of impact as a motivational driver; pay attention to that!).

The people who counsel you probably have the best intentions in the world. They're telling you what they know. That's good! Listen to their counsel. But check it against the way *you* are designed. Maybe relationships don't have the same importance for you as for them; you're more interested in ideas. Maybe you're not naturally inclined to haggle; you'd prefer to just get to know someone. Maybe you're not particularly concerned with changing the world; you just want to understand the social networks of cities.

Mentors know what has worked for them. But the best mentors are the ones who can help you see what works best for you.

FAIL FACTOR #8: ISOLATION

One final "fail factor" that can keep you stuck on the launching pad is trying to figure all of this out on your own. Just as most people need a modeling individual, as described above, most people require a team or community to accomplish anything of significance—including the pursuit of a vision for their life.

The myth of the self-made person is just that—a myth. Even heroes require a supporting cast. The Lone Ranger had Tonto. Matt Dillon had Festus, Kitty, and Doc. Eliot Ness had the Untouchables. Andy Griffith had Barney Fife. Frodo had Sam, along with seven other members of the Fellowship of the Ring. Jack Sparrow had his fellow pirates. Even Lassie had Timmy.

In short, most important achievements are accomplished by teams of people working together. So what makes you think you can figure out what to do with your life on your own? I can think of at least seven different advantages to enlisting other people in your personal "odyssey":

WHY YOU NEED A TEAM

ENCOURAGEMENT
You can always use someone in your corner.

AFFIRMATION
You have people to bring you back to the "good truth" about yourself.

CREATIVITY
You get the benefit of other people's imagination working on your behalf.

WISDOM
You multiply your smarts because others see what you can't see.

NETWORKS
You have potential access to all the people your team knows.

ACCOUNTABILITY
You tend to follow through when you know others are pulling for you.

PRAYERS
You have others believing even when you're doubting.

You need a team. You weren't made to do life on your own. God sometimes uses solitude, but He never uses isolation.[10]

PART III

WHAT DIFFERENCE
DOES IT MAKE?

GIFTEDNESS AND YOUR WORK

I've been talking a lot about how every person was born to do something, something that proves deeply satisfying and expresses their essential personhood.

But you'd never know that looking at the workforce today. Since 2000, the Gallup organization has been tracking what it calls "employee engagement" among workers worldwide. Here are the findings for American workers as of the end of 2012:[1]

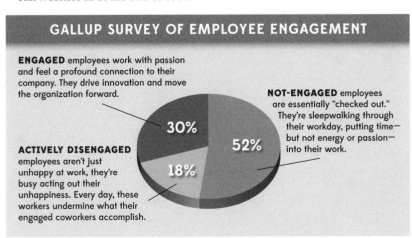

GALLUP SURVEY OF EMPLOYEE ENGAGEMENT

ENGAGED employees work with passion and feel a profound connection to their company. They drive innovation and move the organization forward.

NOT-ENGAGED employees are essentially "checked out." They're sleepwalking through their workday, putting time—but not energy or passion—into their work.

ACTIVELY DISENGAGED employees aren't just unhappy at work, they're busy acting out their unhappiness. Every day, these workers undermine what their engaged coworkers accomplish.

30%

18%

52%

This is scary! More than two-thirds of today's workforce feels no personal stake in their jobs. Fifty-two percent are just marking time. And 18 percent are actively working counterproductively!

What accounts for that? I believe it's because most people are in jobs that don't fit them very well. They are doing work they can do but are not born to do. When you're doing what you're born to do, you put your heart into the job. You love doing it. Yes, there may be things about the job you can't stand—your boss, a coworker, the commute, the travel, the paperwork, compliance issues, stuff like that. But if the job itself matches what you're born to do, you gain satisfaction from doing it. In fact, that satisfaction is what allows you to hang in there despite the bad stuff at work. Let's examine that in more detail.

JOB-FIT

When we talk about giftedness and your work, we're talking about *job-fit*. Everyone wants a job that fits them. But what exactly do we mean by "fit"?

Job-fit has to do with the relative match between you and the actual job you are being asked to do. That's where your giftedness comes into play. Big-time!

Let me explain how this works using a rather simple diagram involving two boxes that overlap to one degree or another.[2] In a way, almost all of my work with people boils down to these two boxes:

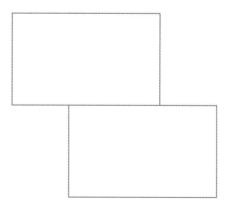

The top box represents you. In that box we put what you *love* to do—"love to do" in the sense of Eric Liddell in *Chariots of Fire*: "God made me fast, and when I run, I feel His pleasure!" Eric Liddell loved to run. He never met a race he didn't want to get into. It was the thing he was born to do.

There's something you are born to do. In chapter 5 I talked about how to figure out what that is. Whatever it is, that's what goes in the top box.

The bottom box represents whatever you're trying to "fit" yourself to, like a job, a career, a role, a position, etc. Like so:

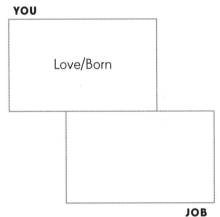

YOU

Love/Born

JOB

Now in order to do an apples-to-apples comparison between you and the job, we have to describe the job in the same motivational language as we describe you. In other words, we have to use the language of giftedness.

Most jobs are not described that way. Most jobs are described by a "job description." (Actually, that's not exactly true. A lot of jobs either have no written job description or else the one they have is out-of-date and/or inaccurate.)

Job descriptions are vitally important. But even when well-crafted, they only list the tasks of the job, *what* is supposed to be done. Behind those tasks, there are always expectations for *how* the job should be done.

Hiring is all about expectations. There are *always* expectations for a job—though often they are not well-articulated. But whoever will be paying you and whoever will be overseeing you have expectations for what "success" in the job looks like. Whatever is required to satisfy those expectations, those are the real motivational requirements of the job:

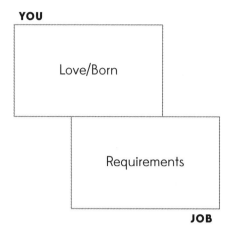

YOU

Love/Born

Requirements

JOB

Let me give an example of what I mean by "motivational requirements." Say you're in sales. Selling may or may not be reflected by your job title, but if your job is to get customers to say yes to spending money with your company, then sales is in your job description.

So what does it actually take to "sell" your particular product or service? In your particular company and industry? In your unique sales environment? What does a person who is succeeding in sales in that arena look like when they are selling? What is it that they are actually doing to get prospects to say yes?

The answers to those questions are the real motivational requirements of the job (at least insofar as the sales part of it goes; there are undoubtedly other aspects to the job affecting the fit). The point is, it's not enough to just look at a job and say it's a "sales" position. You have to ask: What does this employer mean by "sales," and how do they expect me to succeed in sales?

Job-fit is about the way you actually go about doing a job, not just an occupational title for the job, or an assumption about how it's supposed to be done. You have to define the bottom box by asking: What behaviors do I need to do, day in and day out, in order to satisfy my employer's expectations, as well as find satisfaction for myself? Because that's what it's going to take to succeed in the job.

So that's the bottom box.

GOOD FIT

Now you can see that to the extent the two boxes overlap, you have a good fit:

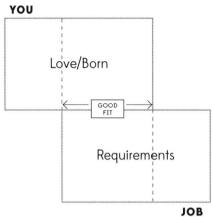

It's a good fit because when you put energy into doing what is required by the job, you actually get a net *gain* of energy back. After all, you're doing something you love to do.

We can illustrate that energy exchange by drawing an arrow from the top box into the bottom box for the energy expended, and another arrow from the bottom box to the top box for the energy gained back:

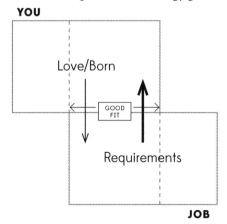

When you're doing what you love to do, you gain energy. You could do it all day long. It doesn't feel like work.

As I've mentioned, my father was a great illustration of that. He was a seminary professor for sixty years at Dallas Theological Seminary. Sixty years at the same institution! Truly amazing. But he loved his work. Indeed, his famous line, always delivered with enormous energy and sincerity, was, "I love to teach! I live to teach! I would teach whether or not they paid me to teach!" Then he'd joke, "Don't tell the seminary that!"

But really it was no joke. The seminary faithfully paid its professors, to be sure—but not much. So Dad never brought home a whole lot of money from teaching. But that didn't matter. He threw himself into teaching with relentless energy and passion.

Moreover, on many a weekend he would get on a plane and go teach at a conference or church somewhere. And here's where I know for a fact that he would teach regardless of the pay: every once in a while, some group didn't pay him. They'd just stiff him! He wasn't happy about that. But Dad was never one to argue about money. So he'd just let it go—and then get right back in front of a group somewhere the next weekend. He genuinely loved to teach!

I've seen doctors, lawyers, bankers, salespeople, counselors, camp directors, musicians, waiters, managers, reporters, harmonica players, wranglers, janitors, concrete workers, homemakers, and yes, even accountants and actuaries who demonstrated a remarkably similar kind of love for their calling.

Good fit can occur for any occupation. Indeed, it *should* occur. There's no reason in the world why it can't occur for anyone, because we now know how to evaluate the top box of a person and the bottom box of a position. The more those two line up, the better the fit. That's what we mean when we say a job "has someone's name on it," or that it "fits them to a tee." It absolutely does, because they're getting paid to do what they love to do.

WHAT DOESN'T FIT?

But now, let me be clear that on this side of heaven, none of us ever gets the "perfect" job. The two boxes never match perfectly. We can get substantial overlap (especially if we're intentional about fit). But we can never get 100 percent overlap.

In the two-box diagram, there are a couple of parts of the boxes that don't overlap. Those are the areas where you and the job don't match.

Notice the right-hand part of the bottom box. Those are things in the position that don't fit you. In other words, the job requires behaviors that you are not naturally motivated to do. But that doesn't matter. Those parts of the job have to get done whether or not you love doing them. So like it or not, you have to do them.

But to do so, you have to extend yourself out into what we call "can-do." You *can* do those things, but you don't love to do them:

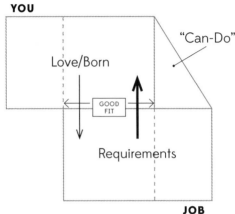

The problem with can-do is that when you put energy into that part of the job, you get no energy back, because you don't love to do that thing. It's a can-do for you, not a love-to-do. So now the arrows of energy only go one way:

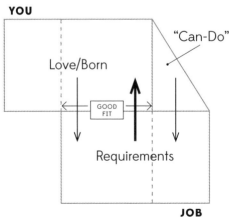

Every job has a certain amount of can-do in it. And that's not altogether bad, because can-do is where your character gets built.

I myself find expense reports to be a real can-do. I worked on a project once where I was doing a lot of travel, and the client's bookkeepers required proof for all expenses before they'd reimburse me. I fought that a couple of times until I woke up and realized, "Hey, Bill, this is not your client's problem, this is your problem! No one's asking you to like filling out expense reports. Just do it—not because you need it (or enjoy it) but because your client needs it." Ever since, I've been reasonably responsible to provide whatever expense reporting someone requires. I still don't like doing it. But that doesn't matter. I can never shirk a responsibility with the excuse, "I don't have to do that because that's outside of my giftedness." No, I always have to be faithful to fulfilling the requirements of the job as best I can.

Okay, so a degree of can-do is actually useful. It's certainly unavoidable. But what you want to avoid is having a whole lot of your job be in the can-do area, like this:

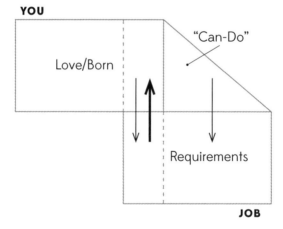

When the match between you and your job looks like that, that's a misfit. That's a big problem! Because you're having to put an enormous amount of energy into the job, but you're getting very little energy back.

I see that scenario almost daily in my practice: individuals with their boxes all out of alignment, or else an employer with an employee whose boxes are out of alignment. Boxes out of alignment create nothing but misery. When you're working at a job that doesn't fit you, you end up hating life:

SYMPTOMS OF POOR JOB-FIT

- You feel a lot of stress.
- You feel bored or disinterested in your work. Your heart isn't in the job.
- You're not very productive, and you make a lot of mistakes.
- You get into lots of conflicts with your boss and/or other employees.
- Your job doesn't make much sense to you. It seems unimportant or pointless.
- You're finding excuses to come to work late or leave early.
- You slack off a lot and/or take long lunches or overly long breaks.
- You feel physical symptoms: headaches, loss of sleep, too much sleep, upset stomach, tension, ulcers, weight gain/loss, hypertension, etc.
- You feel emotional symptoms: frustration, anger, depression, sadness, hopelessness, burnout, etc.
- You wake up Mondays, saying, "Do I have to go to work again?"

Now I realize many people would say the list above is just signs of laziness. I disagree. The issue isn't one of character but of motivation. Because if you're so unmotivated by your job that you're finding excuses for not doing it, then that's a job that doesn't have your name on it. By contrast, when you're in a good job-fit, you genuinely love to do what your employer and/or customer wants you to do, so motivation isn't an issue. If anything, we have to set boundaries to keep you from doing the job too much, because you love it so.

How do so many people end up in jobs that don't fit? The ways are endless! Most of them boil down to ignorance and/or not paying attention: ignorance about what's in the two boxes, or else not paying attention to what is known about them.

But please understand: if you're in a bad job-fit, that does not make you a bad person. Nor, for that matter, does it make your employer a bad employer. A bad job-fit just means you're not fulfilling the real expectations that your employer has for your job because those expectations are asking you to come across with stuff you don't naturally possess.

So when it comes to a poor job-fit, there's no need for either blame or shame. Blame says, "There's something wrong with my employer!" Shame says, "There's something wrong with me!" But job-fit says,

"There's actually nothing 'wrong,' except that someone's trying to put a square peg in a round hole."

PAYCHECK OR PAYOFF?

When your heart is not in your work, you may do the job well enough to satisfy your employer ("can-do" doesn't mean you can't do that part of the job well; you may do it quite well). But once you've done that, you're done, motivationally speaking. You have little if any emotional investment in the job. The only thing that keeps you going back is the money.

Money can get you into all kinds of trouble when it comes to job-fit. Remember the woman I mentioned in the last chapter, who said she hated her job and had quit three times, but kept going back because they kept offering more money? When you're expending significant energy at work but getting very little back, the energy to keep you in the job has to come from somewhere. In most cases, it comes from your employer in the form of money. Money is a powerful motivator. But it's an external motivator. So even if it's able to bind you to the job, it doesn't refresh your soul.

By contrast, if you love your job, you actually don't need to get paid more to do it (recall my dad). Yes, you need to get paid. You need to earn a living. But humans don't actually work just for a paycheck. We're looking for a pay*off*: we're seeking rewards from our work that go way beyond the monetary.

For one person, that payoff is the satisfaction of getting someone else to respond with a yes. For another, it's the joy of standing back and seeing a finished product. For someone else, it's the feeling that comes from outlasting the competition and coming away with the prize. For someone else, it's the exhilaration of seizing upon the answer to a question they've been working on for two or three years.

Payoff is different for every person. Whatever it is for you, you'll pursue it because attaining it makes you feel like you were put on the planet for a reason. You instinctively pursue the pleasure God designed you to enjoy—the satisfaction, the desire, the reward. You want meaning. You want to know that your life counts. You want to feel that there's a purpose for your being in this world. It's very hard to do that if the only thing that keeps you at your job is the money.

WHO IS RESPONSIBLE FOR GOOD JOB-FIT?

It would be wonderful if all the employers in our economy understood the dynamics of job-fit and took extreme measures to ensure that every employee was matched up with a job that had their name on it. They ought to. I think they're wasting money if they don't. But realistically, that's not going to happen. Certainly there are some enlightened employers out there who are unusually altruistic in dealing with their people in this regard. But don't ask me for a list of those companies, because it's a very short list.

> An employer's primary concern is not with you but with the job.

Still, many, if not most, employers understand the importance of putting the right people in the right seats. So why don't they? Look at the diagram again.

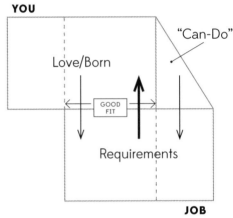

Which of the two boxes is an employer most concerned about? The bottom box, of course. An employer's primary concern is not with you but with the job. The employer has a vested interest in that job getting done. Sure, maybe they'd like you to enjoy doing that job, maybe even love it. But frankly, an employer doesn't care whether you like your job or not. All they care about is that the job gets done, and that it gets done reasonably well.

So, then, which of the two boxes is your main concern? The top box. Because that's your personhood. That's where your giftedness resides. That's what gives you energy and feeds your soul.

To me, that's the most serious aspect of a poor job-fit. Let me speak directly to you if you're in that boat. Yes, it's unfortunate that your employer is not getting the best out of you because you're not in the right job. That's a shame. But the real tragedy if you're in a misfit is that *you* are being diminished. Your personhood is being dishonored. It's being unused. It's being ignored. Here is this beautiful, amazing thing that God, from eternity, envisioned exclusively to reside in you and to be expressed by you, and that thing is just languishing in a lousy job that you don't even care about, except for the money.

What's more, the rest of us are missing out on what God placed you here to offer.

So whose responsibility is it to make sure you're in a good job-fit? Ultimately yours. Because it's your life. It's your job-fit. You have to manage your career. Your employer won't do that for you, nor should they. Your employer is responsible for the bottom box, but you alone are responsible for your top box.

FINDING A JOB YOU CAN LOVE

How, then, do you go about finding a bottom box to match your top box? The steps for doing that have been described by many people before me. But here's a four-stage model to describe the process that almost all experts on this subject recommend:

YOU

your giftedness

STEP 1
Figure out what your
giftedness is.

VISION

STEP 2
Use your giftedness to create
a vision for your life.

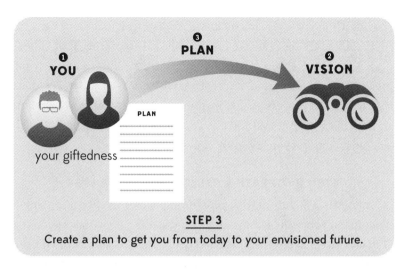

STEP 3
Create a plan to get you from today to your envisioned future.

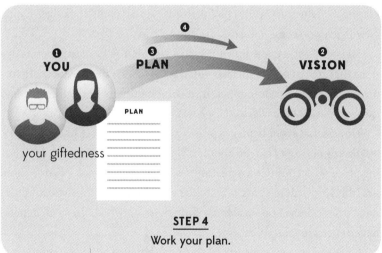

STEP 4
Work your plan.

Let's take these in turn. (You can find more resources for working these steps at the Giftedness Center's website.)

STEP 1: DETERMINE YOUR GIFTEDNESS

If I haven't convinced you already, you really must nail down what your giftedness is all about. Everything depends on that. Recall the two-box diagram. If you don't know what your giftedness is, you can't know what to put in the top box. Which means you can't figure out the bottom box, because your ideal bottom box is a mirror image of whatever is in the top box.

In the back of the book is a process called "Discovering Your Giftedness: A Step-by-Step Guide." If you came to see me, that's essentially the process I would use to find out what your top box is all about. You don't have to use that process. As I've mentioned, there are other assessments around. But whatever tool you use, don't even think about finding a job you can love unless you first know how you are designed.

STEP 2: CREATE A VISION FOR YOUR LIFE

A *vision* is a picture of what your life might look like at some point in the future if you really trust your giftedness, lean into it, make good use of it, and give it every advantage and opportunity. You can't predict the future—except that you *can* predict that your giftedness will still be operating. So why not create a picture for what that could look like? Doing so will give you something to start shooting for.

So how do you come up with such a vision? You have to generate options that at least on the surface would seem to fit your giftedness. There's no exact science for doing that. It's a combination of brainstorming and throwing stuff at the wall to see what sticks.

Now if that sounds messy or less precise than you'd like, I'm sorry, but there's nothing I can do about it. You see, the world is a very interesting place, with countless opportunities for your giftedness. No one could possibly know all of those possibilities. And many of those possibilities don't even exist yet because the technologies on which they will depend haven't been invented yet.

Creating options starts by taking a hard look at what you discovered in step 1 and asking, What are the most prominent features of my giftedness? What have I got to work with here? In plain English, what is it that I keep doing?

For example, let's say that I looked at my giftedness and said, "Hmmm, I really enjoy working with pictures and paints and ink and colors. I do seem to have a good eye for layout and design. I have a history of being drawn to projects where I can blend a lot of elements together into a pleasing visual whole."

What sort of vision could I create from that? Well, one possibility is:

"To create visual art that grabs the eye and makes a point."

Another might be: *"To help someone who has something to say, say it visually."*

Or this: *"To produce a work of art that ends up adorning the lobby of a corporate headquarters, becomes the cover art for a bestselling book, or ends up on the front of* Rolling Stone *magazine."*

Do you see how that works? You start with your giftedness and then describe what you would actually be doing if you used it on a daily basis. Then you *imagine* (key word) a picture of yourself doing that, one that is big enough to inspire you, but not so specific that it limits you or puts you in a box.

A vision is a North Star that guides your path. It keeps you aligned with your giftedness.

I stress this point because if you're trying to find a job or thinking about changing jobs, your focus is probably on your next job. Well, that next job is important, but it needs to fit into a much larger picture of where your life is headed. Otherwise, you're liable to jump from job to job with no real direction. Your next job needs to put you one step closer to your ultimate vision.

Creating Career Scenarios

But of course you have to generate some meaningful options for getting started in that vision—options that pay. I'll say more about giftedness and getting paid in a moment, but how do you translate your giftedness into a job?

I suggest creating what I call "career scenarios." A career scenario is a brief, fifteen- to twenty-word descriptor of what you would look like in a real-world setting if you were using your giftedness. A career scenario is not the same as an occupational title (salesperson, locksmith, software designer, etc.) but rather a bridge between your giftedness and an occupational title.

To create career scenarios, start with some key elements that you know about your giftedness. List those out on a piece of paper: the *abilities* you naturally use; the *things* you enjoy working with; the *environment* or conditions where you seem to do your best stuff; the *roles* you prefer to play. Then start mixing and matching those elements together into sentences to see what they look like when combined.

For example, say you came up with the following elements:

WHAT I KNOW ABOUT MY GIFTEDNESS

ABILITIES
- Figure things out
- Work with my hands
- Challenge/influence others

I WORK WITH
- Materials (lumber, paint, etc.)
- Tools
- Machines
- Logistics
- Groups

CONDITIONS
- Goals
- Challenges
- Outdoors
- Projects
- With a team
- Something with a cause

ROLE
- Independent

Here are some possible combinations of those elements:

- *I'm born to work outdoors with a team, using my hands and working with tools and equipment for something that's a cause.*

- *I'm born to handle the logistics for a group of people working on a challenging project in an outdoors setting.*

- *I'm born to figure out problems related to materials, tools, and machines for a team that handles outdoor projects for some sort of mission or cause.*

- *I'm born to challenge and influence a team working on projects in the outdoors that involve materials, tools, and logistics.*

This process is kind of like shuffling a deck of cards. There are no right or wrong combinations, because all the elements are part of what you naturally do and are born to do. By playing with them in this way, you begin to stimulate your imagination.

For example, take the first collection of elements above: "I'm born to work outdoors with a team, using my hands and working with tools and equipment for something that's a cause." Outdoors is easy enough to picture. What sort of teams work outdoors? Construction crews, work crews, maintenance crews, power company crews, military units, etc. Tools and equipment seem pretty obvious. But what about something that's a cause? That might suggest a nonprofit relief agency, a camp for disadvantaged youth, a ranch that does equine therapy, etc.

So one career scenario that might spring from that brainstorming exercise could be: "To head up work crews for an international nonprofit agency that does construction work overseas."

Another could be: "To work with a crew of roustabouts drilling wells for impoverished communities in Africa."

Yet a third might be: "To handle the operational logistics (materials, equipment, tools, etc.) for an organization building houses in an inner-city community (e.g., Habitat for Humanity)."

What about you? You might want to set the book down for now and see if you can develop some career scenarios for your own giftedness. Doing so will help you start translating what you are wired to do into a job that actually contributes to the world in a meaningful way.

Informational Interviews

So how do you know whether a given option would actually work for you? You may have never considered it before. In fact, you may know nothing about it. Someone else thinks it's a good idea, but how can you be sure? There's only way: you have to get information about that option. And the best information comes from someone who is already doing that option. You have to locate such a person and conduct what is called an *informational interview*.

At the Giftedness Center's website, you'll find a free white paper on how to set up and conduct an informational interview. But I can summarize the process in three steps: (1) locate someone who is actually doing the job you're interested in or is similar to the job you're interested in; (2) contact that person and arrange to meet with them; and (3) conduct the interview and thank them for their help.

The key to this approach is that you are not—repeat not—looking for a job, you're looking for *information*. That makes all the difference in the world. If you approach someone looking for a job, they won't have any time for you. But if you approach them looking for information, they'll tend to be rather accommodating.

The paper explains all the details involved in this process. It's actually a fun adventure in which you meet some really interesting people. But there are enough pitfalls to it that you really owe it to yourself to get the paper and use it as a guide. You don't want something blowing up in your face and harming your reputation.

Once you learn firsthand from someone who is actually doing the kind of work that you're thinking about doing, you'll know pretty quickly whether that work is something you want to pursue. If so, you'll also have a pretty good idea of what it's going to take to get there.

Which brings us to the third stage of the process.

STEP 3: CREATE A PLAN

It's not enough to have a dream for where you want to go. You have to define what it will take to get there. As I just said, the best experts on that are people who are doing what you are interested in doing. Much if not most of your plan should become obvious from your informational interviews.

Every person's plan will be different. The exact elements of your plan depend on your vision and the option you've decided to pursue. But let me mention some areas to consider. Your plan might need to include:

- getting some experience.
- learning a new skill or cultivating one you already have.
- pursuing additional education or training.
- getting some sort of degree, certification, or credential.
- putting a team together.
- putting some money together.
- paying off some debt first.
- learning a foreign language.
- forming a relationship or a set of relationships.
- getting your kids raised.

Again, you'll have to decide what goes in your plan. But whatever that plan involves, you *must* develop it, for two important reasons. The first is that, obviously, nothing is going to happen without it. An intention without a plan is a fantasy. If all you have is a fantasy, don't even bother telling anyone about it, because as soon as they ask how you're going to get there, they'll know you're blowing smoke.

A plan puts legs on your intentions. It gives you a set of marching orders to follow. Instead of just dreaming, you're *doing* something productive aimed at the accomplishment of your vision.

But there's an even more important reason to formulate a plan: it transforms the way you think about yourself. Instead of living with intentions, you start living with intentionality. There's a huge difference! Intentionality means you've accepted who you fundamentally are and have committed to acting on it.

The classic case of that in my work was a nineteen-year-old woman whose giftedness fit her perfectly for acting. If anyone was born to act, she was. I remember one time we were meeting at a Starbucks. I asked her to describe how she was able to portray a character in a role. She pointed to someone who appeared to be a graduate student and made a few observations about him. Then, right in front of me, she *became* that person! She took on his persona. It was spooky!

The question she had brought to me that day was, "How can I explain to people that I'm an actress, when all I'm doing is working odd jobs?"

I said, "But you already are an actress." She shot me a puzzled expression. So I continued, "Look, isn't it true that you have supreme giftedness for inhabiting a role? You just showed me that you do. And isn't it true that you've been onstage since you were four? And isn't it true that you've actually acted in countless productions throughout junior high and high school? And isn't it true that you've actually gotten paid for a minor part in a movie, as well as for quite a few modeling jobs?" She affirmed each of my questions with a nod.

"Then there's nothing to explain," I concluded. "You're an actress. You've always been an actress. Your vision is to continue to be an actress. You're an actress! So the next time someone asks, 'What do you do for work?' you say, 'I'm an actress.' And when they say, 'Oh, how interesting.

Where are you acting now?' you say, 'Well, right now I'm between projects. So my day job is waiting tables (or whatever). But I look forward to seeing what the next project turns out to be.' That's a totally plausible narrative. And totally true!"

That woman had never seen herself that way. She had been among the vast majority of people who think their identity is defined by their current occupation instead of their giftedness. Locked in that mindset, their dreams, or intentions, remain just that—intentions.

As a result of our conversation that day, that woman began to see herself as an actress, with the result that she began living like an actress and doing the things actresses do. Yes, she continued to work odd jobs. But she had started to live intentionally. Will she end up onstage or in a film? I have no idea. Neither does she. But she wouldn't trade living intentionally for one moment of living desperately (which is how Henry David Thoreau characterized the lives of most people[3]).

When you live with intentionality, you have a purpose. You're on a mission. You *select* where you devote your energy. You don't just live randomly or passively. You can't control the future or what happens to you. But you can head in the direction of your North Star, regardless of whether life cooperates. Sometimes it won't. But oftentimes it will. Such appears to be how God has constructed this world. By faithfully putting one step after another in that direction over time, the odds are—and the experiences of countless humans who have preceded you confirm it— that you *will* achieve some semblance of your vision. I can't explain it. It's a mystery. But why not just go with it?

STEP 4: WORK YOUR PLAN

A plan does no good unless you act on it. Occasionally I have a corporate client ask me to diagnose their troubles and then devise a plan for solving them. I do so. I submit the plan. They pay me. Then the plan goes in a file drawer. Nothing changes. How silly is that?

No more silly than if you come up with a plan for what it will take to achieve your vision, and then fail to act on it.

Acting on your plan is where things get tough because they get real. It's not easy to get that graduate degree (if that's what you need to accomplish your vision). It takes time and effort to get that experience (if that's what you need). You'll get turned down ten or twenty or thirty times before you get that book contract you need to secure (if that factors into your plan).

To be sure, not all plans are tough. Sometimes things just fall into place. But the point is, a plan is on paper, whereas working your plan involves real energy expended. The good news is that if you have a vision (which gives you hope and direction) and you're acting according to your giftedness (which gives you energy), it's actually fun to work your plan, because you can see it taking shape right before your very eyes.

And working your plan turns out to be far more interesting than it appears. You see, when you actually take steps toward the achievement of your vision, you discover that God is working behind the scenes in ways you could never have foreseen.

For example, when I was graduating from high school in 1972, suppose someone had said to me, "Bill, whatever you do, roll China into your thinking." At the time, China was a sworn enemy of the United States. So that would be like me telling you that North Korea is going to be the next big thing.

"Oh no, Bill," my imagined advisor continues. "In a few short years, China will be a major trading partner with the United States. Why, they'll have embraced a form of capitalism. In fact, some of the people you're in school with right now will be living and working in China. Believe it or not, you're going to get married and have three daughters, and one of them will have been to China and back twice before she graduates from high school."

I would have called that person absolutely crazy! And yet, all of that has come true.

If your giftedness were just your own private affair, all the burden would be on you to make it come to pass. But your giftedness is not all on you. It doesn't even derive from you. It's a gift from God. And what you discover is that God is at work in ways you can't even fathom, orchestrating events in the world such that where you end up may turn out to be in a place very different from where you originally imagined—and perhaps way beyond what you could have ever imagined.

CALIBRATING YOUR EXPECTATIONS

I want to do everything I can to encourage you to lean into your gift-edness and accomplish your vision. But I also want to inject some realism into your expectations for how this process works.

Based on everything I've said, you would think that once you figure out your giftedness and define a career option that fits it, all you have to do is look in the classified ads or go on Monster.com and find that job. In one fell swoop, you could jump from a poor job-fit to your "perfect" job, like this:

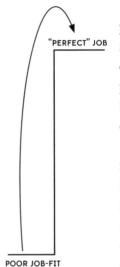

And yet, in all the years that I've been helping people figure out their life and career directions—nearly two decades—that's never happened for one person. Not one! Which says that either my process doesn't work, or it doesn't work that way. I'm convinced it's the latter, based on the experience of hundreds of people.

If you're in a poor job-fit, or if you're looking for a job, you know you have to do something. So you look at the options at hand, and probably none of them is your "perfect" job. But that doesn't matter. Finding the best job-fit is not the best fit conceivable but the best fit *achievable,* given the options. So you pick the option that seems to fit with your giftedness better than the others, and you go with it. Like this:

Again, this is far from your ideal job. But it's at least a somewhat better fit than what you had before.

Now the key at this point is not to just settle. You don't say, "Well, I guess this is as good as it gets. Bill got me all fired up to find my dream job, but that didn't happen. I must not be one of the fortunate ones." No! You lean into that job and do good work, but you keep scanning the horizon for a better option. Inevitably one will come along. When it does, you take it and move up the ladder of fit:

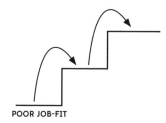

This is an important move, because now you're using more of your giftedness in your work. And when that happens, you're more productive and you do better work. That leads to success, and with success comes better opportunities. Inevitably one of those opportunities will be a much better fit, and so you move farther up the ladder:

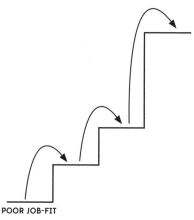

By this process, I've seen countless people work their way into better and better job-fits, until one day they contact me and say something along the lines of, "Bill, I never thought it would happen to me, but I feel like I'm in the perfect job for me!"

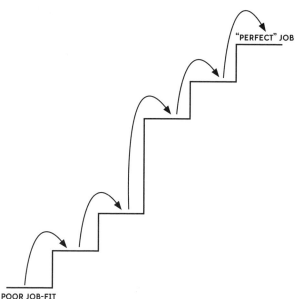

How long does this process take? I'd say five to seven years, on average. In a handful of cases it's gone faster than that. But even if it took ten or twenty years, wouldn't it be worth every minute of the journey to finally land in a job that makes excellent use of your giftedness?

DON'T TRY THIS BY YOURSELF!

I concluded the last chapter with a warning about the "fail factor" of isolation. That warning bears repeating here. If there's any reason why the process I've described here ends up not working for you, it will be because you'll try to do it by yourself.

It won't be because the process is too hard. I sometimes hear that criticism: "Bill, this looks like an awful lot of work! Isn't there a faster, easier way?" Yes, there are faster and easier ways. None of them has yet proven to be very effective. And some of them will get you into real trouble. None of them is robust enough to change the game for where your life is headed.

The process I'm describing can indeed change your life. I wouldn't call it easy, but I also wouldn't call it impossible. It requires some effort, but it's not brain surgery. It's something anyone can do, the way anyone can learn to fly-fish, or work out, or become proficient at using a computer. Indeed, it's a new skill to acquire. Call it the skill of intentionally living out your giftedness.

When I compare the people who have worked this process and ended up in their sweet spot, versus the ones who have not worked it and therefore languished, the key variables are a *coach* and a *team*. The people who enlist a guide and a community invariably make progress. The people who don't do this usually don't make progress. It's that simple.

Where do you find a coach? The answer is, again, from among your network. Somewhere in your network is someone who will agree to meet with you periodically—once a week, once every couple of weeks, once a month, or whenever. The point is, you're going to tell this person that you're embarking on a journey related to your life and career, and you would value their support as you pursue that journey, especially in the early going.

What's the coach's role? (And by the way, you don't have to formally call them your coach, or mentor, or guide, or any other term. Lots of the people I coach just say, "I meet with Bill." Enough said.)

Your coach is there to give you a vote of confidence. To believe in you. To affirm your intentionality by lending you a bit of their time. To keep bringing you back to the truth about yourself (your giftedness). To listen to you and allow you to reveal your heart, as well as express your feelings. To ask questions you haven't thought of asking. To lend perspective to your experience and perceptions. To provide whatever wisdom they have about your situation. To suggest steps and ideas you haven't considered. To help you follow through on what you've said you're going to do (that's called accountability). To celebrate your successes and help you through your disappointments. To pray for you, and if you're open to it, with you.

You may be wondering whether anyone like that actually exists. Yes they do, and in fact they're everywhere. They're a lot closer than you think. On the surface, some of them may not appear to have much to offer because they're a bit different from you. They may be your parents' age. They may come from a very different background. They may have a lot more education than you. Or they may have less education but a lot more wisdom and experience than you.

In short, there's a coach out there somewhere for you. "All" you have to do is take the initiative of asking them to meet you for coffee, and then telling them you're looking for some moral support as you navigate toward your vision. The right person will almost always agree to help you out, because the quintessential trait of the right person is that they care. They're not just about their own life and concerns. They genuinely want to see another person thrive. There's no reason why that person can't be you.

(By the way, many people reading this book have what it takes to coach someone along the lines I'm describing. For more on that, see the brief section in the back of the book entitled "You Could Be a Giftedness Coach.")

Meanwhile, you also need to recruit a handful of companions who will agree to simply walk alongside you. If it's going to take you five to seven years to get from today to that ideal job-fit tomorrow, you're going to need some relationships that will stick with you for the long haul.

I'm not just talking about acquaintances. I'm talking about people who really do care what happens to you. These are folks you're willing to confide in, to tell about possible opportunities, and to notify when new developments take place in your journey. When you have that kind of support around you, you're going to be a lot more confident and more willing to take risks. And when disappointments come, you're going to be in a better position to handle them because you know that no matter what, you've got some people in your corner.

WHAT ABOUT THE MONEY PART?

"Bill, this giftedness thing sounds great. What you're saying makes a lot sense. But let's get practical. I've got to get paid. I've got to earn a living. I can't afford to play around trying to find the perfect job. Maybe once I've got a salary or whatever, I'll have the luxury of bothering with my giftedness. But it just sounds idealistic to think everyone can get paid to do what they love to do."

> The big mistake most people make is trying to figure out how to get paid instead of how to create value.

I've heard that objection a thousand times! It's the idea that giftedness is a luxury. It's something a few independently wealthy people might be able to enjoy, or a tiny fraction of celebrity athletes, musicians, artists, and other fortunate lottery winners get to indulge. The rest of us have to find whatever job we can find that pays. Whether we like it or not is beside the point. (And those push backs are just from people in the United States, where we have lots of options. Imagine what I've heard from people in other parts of the world who have few if any options for work!)

That mindset is so widespread that for me to insist otherwise is like spitting in the wind. But I do so anyway. I have no choice, because giftedness is not a luxury, it's a reality. It's just the way the world is, the way humans are. We can ignore that—and obviously most people in the world, including leaders in industries and governments, have ignored it, or at least not been aware of it. The result has been a colossal mess! But that doesn't mean giftedness isn't real or doesn't "work." Nor does it mean that it's impractical. When used and honored, it becomes *very* practical.

Indeed, giftedness is the means by which humans create value. Remember, your giftedness didn't just happen. It was given to you by God. That alone means it's not a luxury. It was given to you for a purpose, to make a contribution to the world (among other reasons). It arms you with a means of creating value.

"Value" means what someone is willing to pay for. People never buy a product or a service, they buy value. People don't buy cars, they buy prestige, or safety, or fuel economy, or affordable transportation, or some other value. Likewise, when someone buys a book, they're not buying the book, they're buying information, or instruction, or inspiration, or an escape, or whatever.

Monetizing your giftedness means finding a way to use it to add value. Do that and you'll get paid. Except the big mistake most people make is trying to figure out how to get paid instead of how to create value. They think it's all about the money. Money's involved, absolutely. But to be hard-boiled about it, the person who pays you doesn't really care about you and what you need. Their main concern is with their task or problem or need or whatever, and whether you can offer something of value to address it. If you make that contribution, you get paid. If not, you don't. And shouldn't!

Bill Gates (no stranger to what it takes to earn money) was told by a college student that growing up her career ambition was to be the richest person in the world. So she wanted know how she could become like Bill Gates. He replied, "I didn't start out with a dream of being super-rich. . . . I think most people who've done well have sort of found something that they just are kind of nuts about doing. Then they figure out a way to hire their friends to do it with them. And if it's in an area of great impact, then sometimes you get sort of financial independence."[4]

What are you nuts about? How can you monetize that by adding value?

Whatever that is, you're going to have to find a customer for it. A customer is someone who needs what you have to offer. Finding that person is what we call marketing. Someone out there actually needs what you've got, or else God wouldn't have given you what you've got. But that person doesn't know about you and what you've got. So you have to vector toward them and help them figure out that you're the answer to their prayer (figuratively speaking, but sometimes literally, as well). Then you have to strike some terms that allow you to supply that value.

Does it sound crude to reduce your giftedness to a financial transaction that is subject to market forces? Get over it! And then get on with it! God didn't set the world up to indulge our fantasies. He set it up to be fruitful and to meet our needs. To that end He's given us work. And to do that work He's given each of us our giftedness. The fact that we love using our giftedness is a bonus, not our purpose. Our giftedness is our particular way of making the world fruitful, of adding value to it. If we do that, we get paid. If not, we don't. And shouldn't!

And what bothers me most is not that we live in a fallen world where some people, because of infirmity, are not able to fully participate in the joy of work. We have to be especially protective of and generous to those folks. And other people, because of unjust economic systems and power structures, are forced to work in ways that are unworthy of human dignity. That vast sector of humanity cries out for freedom and justice.

No, what bothers me most are people who have abundant options for exploring where and how they might use their giftedness productively, and yet default to any old job they can find, just because it pays. They just assume they can never get paid to do what they love to do. They have no faith in their gift! Apparently God didn't understand how the world works when He gave it to them. They just settle. Then they turn around and wonder why their work seems so boring or insignificant or bothersome or toilsome, and why their life feels so pointless and uninspired.

Bill Gates's lifelong competitor, Steve Jobs, told the 2005 graduating class at Stanford, "You've got to find what you love. . . . Your work is going to fill a large part of your life, and the only way to be truly satisfied is to do what you believe is great work. And the only way to do great work is to love what you do. If you haven't found it yet, keep looking. Don't settle."[5]

That could easily have been the title for this book, or at least this chapter. *Don't settle!*

THE BEST FIT ACHIEVABLE

I'm more aware than anyone about the challenges facing you if you're trying to find a job that fits you. It's one thing to tell Stanford graduates to keep looking for work they love and not settle. Those people are really bright and have options. You may not be as fortunate. But then, good fortune is overrated: even Stanford (and Harvard) graduates have to contend with work world realities that simply don't care what anyone loves to do. It is truly a tough world out there!

So even as I implore you to seek diligently for a good job-fit, I mean the best fit *achievable*, not the best fit conceivable. Anyone can fantasize about their dream job. Get paid a million dollars a year or more to just do whatever you love doing under ideal circumstances and with complete flexibility? Yeah, who wouldn't want that? But the wakeup alarm goes off at 5:00 tomorrow morning, and the real world summons you.

That world is a mess compared to what was originally intended. When any of us seeks to apply our gifts in doing meaningful work through a job that fits us, we have to subject our giftedness to that mess.

> We still know very little about educating masses of people to do knowledge work.

One daunting part of the mess is a global oversupply of workers, which some believe may be permanent, given the relentless advances of technology. Is a machine now doing a job you used to do? Did your job get sent overseas to a cheaper labor market? Hold on! Whatever disruptions our ways of working have undergone in the past ten or twenty years are nothing compared to what some economists think will happen in the next ten to twenty years.[6] Could an app be in development that's going to replace you?

Needless to say, the value and importance of education, both foundational and ongoing, will skyrocket in the coming years. Quite simply, the more education one has, the more and better options they will have. Giftedness may be inborn, but it still has to be developed into marketable skills. We still know very little about educating masses of people to do knowledge work. But who says that can't change? To my mind, figuring that out may be the biggest opportunity of this century and yield incalculable benefits.

A greater and darker challenge to surmount is the many injustices and abuses of power in the work world. Broken and even evil structures and systems create untold misery for countless workers. The interlocking ways that societies are set up often make it seem almost impossible for people to use their gifts effectively *and* make a living. What gets rewarded is keeping the system going. And so the values are all messed up. If you can manage, sell, or make things deemed "useful," you get rewarded, often handsomely. But if your giftedness is about "soft" activities like nurturing or making the world beautiful, you may barely be able to get by—and maybe not at all.

It's one thing to contend with these realities when you're young and healthy. But what if you're not? I know a man who took over as CEO of an organization, only to be told six months later that he had life-threatening cancer and, in all likelihood, months to live. He regretfully tendered his resignation and submitted to the gruesome gauntlet of therapies prescribed for him. Beyond all expectation, he survived. Then six months later a rare complication of the therapy struck his body. Again he was told his chances were marginal. Miraculously, he survived. After a year of recuperation, he's resumed his search for work that fits him, but he's now chronically hampered by the permanent effects of what he's been through.

These are very difficult questions, and in this book I can't begin to address them adequately. But I think the simplest answer goes back to what I just said: the "best-fitting" job means the best fit achievable, not the best fit conceivable. I could point to extreme cases of people in the most dire straits who seemingly had *no* options[7] yet managed to express their giftedness nonetheless. Remember, your giftedness is irrepressible. You cannot not express it. But you can also give in to "the way things are" and choose to simply ignore it.

Does giftedness always have to be expressed through paid work? Of course not. But look at it this way. The work of the world has to be done. It just makes sense that it be done by people who are gifted to the task. So if you're going to work anyway, you might as well seek work that fits. The best available option may not be a job that fits you all that well, but in the long run it makes more sense to take it than to settle for another job that doesn't fit you nearly as well.

I concede that in this broken world, you may not be able to make a living doing your particular giftedness. If not, you'll need to make a living doing something else. *But just because society may not value your giftedness enough to pay you for it doesn't exempt you from honoring, cultivating, and findings ways to express it.* As my dad used to say, "Your career is what you're paid to do. Your calling is what you're made to do." You were made to do "good works." Nothing says that all of those good works will pay. In fact, many of the best works the world has ever seen were not paying gigs, but fortunately, people did them anyway. How did those people survive while doing those things for free? They essentially "waited tables" and/or lived off charity. They did with less. But not because they settled!

Even within bad systems, people still manage to use their giftedness and make contributions. The possibilities are never black-and-white. And some people's giftedness is actually ideal for trying to bring about changes in bad systems. Think of William Wilberforce taking on slavery, or Martin Luther King Jr. leading the civil rights movement.

Even the smallest expressions of giftedness, whether made inside or outside economic systems, are I think one of God's incredible graces that enable us to bear up under the awful, entrenched mess that human culture so often becomes.

Consider Nkosi Johnson, a South African boy of twelve who died of AIDS in 2001. Born HIV-positive, he never knew his father and was given up for adoption when his ailing mother could no longer care for him. Yet assisted by his foster mother, he started Nkosi's Haven, a refuge for HIV-positive mothers and their children in Johannesburg. He aspired to grow up and become a speaker and educator on AIDS. But he didn't settle for "someday." He lived each day he was given by following the creed, "Do all you can with what you have in the time you have in the place you are."[8]

HOMEMAKING

One group of workers that merits special attention here is homemakers. An entire book could be written on the tie-ins between giftedness and homemaking. This is such a touchy topic! And I'm at a disadvantage because I'm a man. But let me just make a quick observation.

First, I salute and celebrate mothers everywhere, whether they have a full-time job, part-time job, or stay at home and don't get paid at all. I especially relate to single moms, having been a single dad myself.

Mothering is a role, a set of expectations—a "bottom box," if you will. For some women that bottom box fits like a glove. But not for all. For some it's actually a terrible fit. For others, the role is actually a great fit, but not one that soaks up all of their motivational horsepower. We see both of those scenarios (among others) all the time at the Giftedness Center.[9]

Where things get confused—and controversial—is over the question of whether a mother should be employed outside the home. A number of issues affect the answer, including what's best for the children, what's best for the mother, and what the family's financial realities are. There are also seasons-of-life angles to what's appropriate, and when. Different families are going to come to different conclusions about that puzzle.

All I know is this: kids seem to be happiest and have the fewest "issues" when their mother seems to be satisfied with how she is spending her life. There is something in the relationship between a mother and her child that the child senses when Mommy is angry, frustrated, upset, distressed, depressed, or resentful; or conversely, when she is enthusiastic, energetic, confident, committed, purposeful, and hopeful. That saw cuts both ways whether the mother has paying work apart from her mothering responsibilities or not.

> In my perfect world, people would find work that fits them and do that until they die.

Some stay-at-home moms love it, are great at it, and their kids can feel it. Other stay-at-home moms are restless and feel "stuck," or feel worthless, like they're not "doing" anything. Their kids can feel that. Is the answer to go get a job? Maybe, especially if it's the right job (one that fits). But not necessarily. Sometimes just knowing what your giftedness is and then finding ways to express it through mothering, as well as through your own personal interests, can turn things around dramatically.

Some mothers in the workforce are doing exactly what they were designed to do, and their kids can feel that, too. As long as the kids' needs are being met and they feel loved, they just accept it as a matter of life that Mommy works. But if Mommy comes home every day worn out and complaining about her job, her boss, and her coworkers, her kids will feel that—and they won't like it. Because they don't want Mommy to feel bad. All kinds of trouble are possible as a result. Should a woman in that situation quit and stay home? Not necessarily. Doing that may actually worsen her troubles. The better course would be to consider finding a better job-fit. But in any case, she needs to understand her innate wiring.

RETIREMENT

I don't think it will come as any surprise that I find the whole notion of retirement questionable. In my perfect world, people would find work that fits them and do that until they die. The exact nature and content of their work might change over the years, but they'd keep using their giftedness all the way to the end.

But the world is not perfect. On the one hand, we have some people retiring with plenty of money, and they plan to spend the rest of their lives doing stuff they never had time for before, like traveling or reading or playing golf. Nothing wrong with those activities, but that's a perilous strategy. Unless you're doing something meaningful, life ends up feeling pretty empty. The only way I know to do something meaningful (as you define it) is to devote yourself to some task that taps into your giftedness.

A lot of other people, especially Boomers, are realizing that they won't be retiring nearly as early as they were planning to, thanks to the vaporization of trillions of dollars in investments and retirement savings over the past few years. Meanwhile, countless people in their sixties and seventies feel like they've never done anything that really fit them. Are they too old to hope that they ever will?

Absolutely not! Every day you're alive, God has a purpose for you being here. Your task is to find and follow that purpose. Trust me, it's linked to your giftedness. As I said earlier, you may not be able to find it much in your paid job, but if not, start looking for it outside of work. Now that your kids are older and out of the home, you've got a lot more margin to work with. Don't waste it! Find a "bottom box" that has meaning for you. It could indeed be a hobby. But it might revolve around volunteer service in your community or at your church. You might even have some little activity you've been doing on the side to make a little spending money, such as knitting scarves, baking cakes, collecting rare books, or making salsa. Is it possible there might potential in that interest now that you have more time to devote to it?

Of course, one huge opportunity (and responsibility) for older people is to help younger generations prepare to take over when you're gone. Any day of the week you can call around and find schools, youth centers and programs, juvenile facilities, and other institutions that will be happy to sign you up to help children learn to read, or to tutor, mentor, or coach them.

And then there's my personal crusade, which is to raise up an army of adults who will form relationships with young adults in the twenties and invite them into the adult world of work. Call it mentoring, coaching, guidance, whatever. In the back of the book, I have a brief description of what it means to be a Giftedness Coach. But if you want to profoundly affect the course of someone's life, I encourage you to use this book as a basis for helping a young adult gain a better understanding of their giftedness and then use that insight to find work that fits them.

Whatever you end up doing in your senior years, make your life count! Maybe it's been a long, hard journey and you're just ready to kick back, relax, and rest. That's fine. A resting person can still be a purposeful person. Indeed, the greatest tonic to the soul is to do what you were designed to do.

Or maybe you've been bored your whole life. Isn't it time to change that? Why assume that your best years can't lie ahead?

At fifty-nine I'm old enough to know people who as young adults played it safe and went for the career that looked like it would pay well, even if it didn't fit them. By midlife they had long since settled into meaningless mediocrity—just marking time, shuffling along through life. Now in their senior years, they're squandering what time they have left. They're not bad people. But I regard them as tragic people. They will "die with all their music still in them."[10]

8

GIFTEDNESS AND
YOUR RELATIONSHIPS

This book is all about you. But if we're going to talk about you, we have to talk about "you *and*." You don't exist in isolation. There are currently 7 billion other people on the planet, some of whom are in your life. So in this chapter I want to talk about you *and* your spouse, you *and* your child, you *and* your parents, you *and* your coworkers, and so on.

The first thing to point out is that just as you have your particular giftedness, every other person has their own particular giftedness. So anytime you and someone else interact, those two forms of giftedness interact. And that's where things get interesting!

THE TWO-BOX DIAGRAM REVISITED

In the last chapter, I illustrated the notion of job-fit using a diagram of two overlapping boxes. We can use that same diagram to illustrate what happens when you and another person deal with each other. Only instead of putting one box on top of the other, we put them side by side, like this:

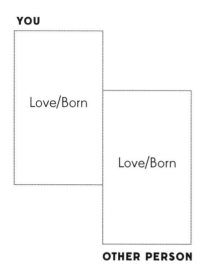

Notice that you instinctively relate to the other person out of what you love to do and are born to do. You can't help it. Indeed, you can't really do it any other way. That's just who you are. It's your personhood.

By the same token, the other person also brings to the relationship what they love to do and are born to do. That's just who they are. It's their personhood.

Now you can quickly see that parts of who you are and parts of who the other person is will overlap to some extent. That is, you'll be compatible. Maybe that's what they call "chemistry," but the point is, some of your giftedness and the other person's giftedness will get along just fine:

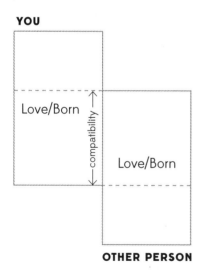

For example, say you're consumed with the world of ideas. You love to read literature, talk philosophy, watch fascinating TED talks, and so forth. When you come across someone with similar interests, you instinctively resonate with that person. The two of you are like peas in a pod. You "get" one another, as they say.

Likewise, say you're a visionary entrepreneur with lots of ideas for your next "big thing." But you're a mess with details, scheduling, logistics, reports, and paperwork. That stuff is just not in your giftedness. Then along comes someone who is the soul of organization and execution. They have a real gift for operations and building systems that create efficiencies and get results. That practical person puts wind under your imaginative wings, and the next thing you know, the two of you are making real progress together. It's a marriage made in heaven!

So sometimes the giftedness all works together. But of course, inevitably there are parts of you and parts of the other person that are not at all in sync:

To continue with the illustration just given, suppose you're faced with making a major decision involving a commitment of time and money. You, being the visionary you are, instinctively want to push full steam ahead and seize the opportunity. But your pragmatic partner is far more cautious. They want to slow down and get more information and think it all through. The clock is ticking, so you're feeling impatient. But the other person has their eye on the potential pitfalls, so they're in no hurry.

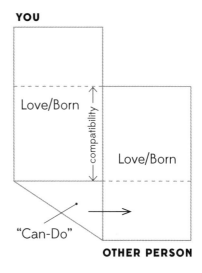

In short, you're now experiencing "can-do" in your relationship with that other person. Remember that "can-do" is energy you have to work up to accomplish something because you aren't instinctively born to do it. "Can-do" is taxing. It drains you. You put energy out, but you get no energy back.

Now, what do you do when someone does things differently than you do? What's your natural reaction? If you're like most people, it's to say (or at least think):

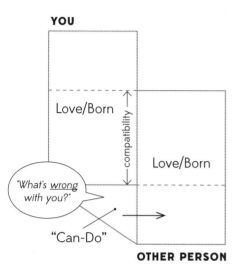

That's just human nature. When someone thinks differently than we think, or values things differently than we do, or does some task in a different way than we would, our natural impulse is to react: "What's wrong with you?!"

Meanwhile, guess what? There are parts of you that the other person finds, well, difficult. To stay with the illustration, your practical minded sidekick has been listening to you come in every day with yet another new idea. At first it seemed interesting, even charming. But after a while, it's proven grating, to say the least. That other person hasn't said this to you, but they're thinking, "Why don't we finish one of the previous fifty-eight ideas you've had this week before we start chasing another one?" In other words, they've got some of their own "can-do" going on relative to you. In their own way, they are also asking the question, "What's wrong with you?!"

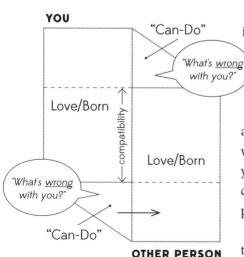

You can see where this is all going. It's a recipe for conflict. And depending on factors such as what else is in your giftedness and the other person's giftedness, how mature the two of you are, and how each of you has dealt with all the previous conflicts you've ever had in your lives, that conflict could be handled well or poorly or not at all.

But notice: When you look at the other person and ask, "What's wrong with you?!," what's the answer to that question? The answer is there's nothing "wrong" with them! They're just being who they are. When that other person keeps stalling you because they need more information in order to have a comfort level with making the decision, they are not trying to be "stubborn," or "timid," or "difficult," or "controlling," or any of the countless other negative labels you may instinctively want to tag them with. No, they are acting that way out of their God-given giftedness, out of the *best* of who they are. They are doing exactly what God designed them to do.

Conversely, when the other person looks at you and says, "What's wrong with you?!," the answer to that question is likewise: there's nothing "wrong" with you. You're not intentionally being "reckless" or "foolhardy" or "wild-eyed" or "impulsive" or any of the countless other negative labels the other person may assign to you. You're just being who God made you to be.

Perhaps you can see why I believe that most of the problems we have in our relationships as human beings do not stem from issues of character, or emotions, or psychology, or morality, or even spirituality, as is commonly assumed. No, they fundamentally begin at a *motivational* level. When two persons interact, their respective forms of giftedness automatically kick into gear, and as long as the gears mesh, things go reasonably well. But when the gears grind, there's friction, heat, and noise!

I'm not saying that issues of character, emotions, psychology, morality, and spirituality don't come into play. They absolutely come into play! If someone is given to lying (a character issue), they're liable to roll some lies into the conflict. If they are afraid (an emotion), they may interact with deep suspicion and mistrust. If they have a psychological condition like schizophrenia or bipolar disorder, that will certainly affect how they handle matters. If they're totally selfish (a spiritual area), they will likely be pretty selfish in the way they behave.

So all that other stuff gets very involved. But everything starts with two people being who they are. They cannot do otherwise.

SEEING PERSONS

I know this way of thinking about people may be radically new or different for some. And some may not buy it at all. That's fine. I'm not saying it's the final word on human interaction. Far from it! People are very complex, and our relationships with one another are even more complex. But I believe the phenomenon of giftedness gives us a baseline for a habit I call "*seeing* the person."

There's a big difference between looking at someone and *seeing* them. If I see you doing something and go, "What's wrong with you?!" I'm looking at you. I'm seeing what doesn't make sense to me, and then forming a conclusion about you: something is "wrong" with you (or so I think).

But suppose I were somehow able to crawl inside your skin and see the world the way you do? What if I could see all the memories you have from throughout your life, and all the experiences you've been through, both good and bad, and all the emotions that you feel and have ever felt, and all the relationships you've ever had? If I could see all of that, then what you're doing would make all the sense in the world. My perceptions (or misperceptions) about you would instantly change. I would actually *see* you as a person.

> We meet someone and immediately start putting them in a box.

Well, of course, I can't crawl inside your skin. And yet . . . thanks to the phenomenon of giftedness, there actually is a way to do that, to *see* you—because your giftedness reveals the heart of your personhood.

So when I interact with you or anyone else, it would help a lot if I tried to understand something about your giftedness—if I suspended judgment and just let you be you for a little bit.

Now let me digress for a moment and say a word about judgment. We humans are nothing if not judgmental. We have all these labels, all these categories and criticisms with which we assault one another. Maybe not out loud, although that happens a lot. But at least in our minds, which amounts to the same thing.

We meet someone and immediately start putting them in a box. "Boy, this fellow's a real dweeb!" "Now isn't she the control freak?" "You're so boring." "Obviously this guy's not going anywhere. No ambition!" "Does she have any idea how dumb she sounds?" "He's so full of himself!" "What asylum did they let this wingnut out of?" "What a loser!"

Look, I'm human and I do the same thing. Except that working with giftedness has hopefully made me do it less and less. I've found that if I can get past first impressions and discover what is under the hood by way of someone's giftedness, I'm almost always shocked at what an unbelievably amazing person they turn out to be. Not that I end up liking everybody. That's unrealistic. But even the ones I can't stand or even detest, I still end up admiring the way God put them together, no matter how twisted they may have become.

And that's what *seeing* persons is all about: seeing them the way God sees them. And how does He see them? Well, in chapter 2 we said that God delights in each person because He sees something of Himself in each one.

"Well, God may delight in them, but I sure don't!" you might respond. "All I see is someone who's a mess, or suspicious, or annoying, or stupid, or mean, or clueless . . . or whatever." (You see how judgment permeates our eyesight.)

God knows all that. He knows that when you look at the average person in this world, you certainly wouldn't guess on the face of it that they represent God. For that very reason, God told Samuel when he was sent to find and anoint a new king over Israel, "The Lord does not look at the things people look at. People look at the outward appearance, but the Lord looks at the heart."[1]

There are a lot of things God sees when He looks at someone's heart, but at the core of their heart is their personhood. God sees how He made that person.[2]

So what happens if you and I start trying to *see* who the person is that we're dealing with? See past their outward appearance, unpleasant attitude, neediness? What if we, in a sense, accepted them on their own terms—keeping healthy boundaries, to be sure, but discovering who they are and allowing them to be that person?

I find that a person's giftedness is extremely valuable for "discovering" another person. For instance, suppose I recognize that at the core you are fundamentally about demonstrating that you are competent and therefore go to great lengths to equip yourself with knowledge and skills, and to carefully prepare before you act. I see that and accept that. If so, I will appreciate why you get terribly frustrated and even angry by something that makes you look incompetent. I will be a bit more patient when you refuse to act because you don't feel prepared. I will understand (even though I won't like it) when you badger me to try something I don't think I can do, because you don't want me to look incompetent.

Seeing the other person will transform your relationships. You will find yourself becoming far more understanding and accepting of others. You will have more patience. You will exhibit more grace and forbearance. You will have more tolerance for people's limitations. You'll have more compassion for their failures and sins. In short, you'll see them the way God sees them. Hopefully, in doing so, you'll end up seeing something beautiful in them, the beauty that God put into them because He wants them to show everyone else how beautiful He is.

The implications of seeing people this way—according to their giftedness—are far-reaching for every one of your relationships. Let's start with your marriage.

GIFTEDNESS AND YOUR MARRIAGE

Lynn and I had been married for about three and a half years, and one day we were reflecting on the challenges of married life. We both agreed that the first year is the hardest. "Yeah," she said, "after I'd been married to you for about a year, I told all my friends, 'I'm surprised the divorce rate is not higher than 50 percent.'"

Needless to say, I make no pretense to being an expert on marriage! I'm just like you and most everybody else (if you're married), trying to do the best I can with limited faculties to love and honor my spouse. It's a tall order.

However, I do think that the two-box diagram offers some insight into the degree of difficulty we're up against in trying to relate to our spouses. Consider the following two marriages. Which one would you say is liable to have more challenges?

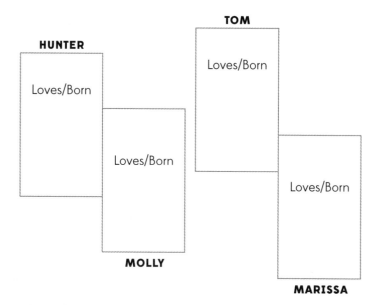

Obviously Tom and Marissa. They see the world very differently through the lenses of their very different giftedness. Each will have to really work at understanding the other. Just look at the amount of "can-do" in their relationship. They can certainly get on the same page and come to unity in their marriage, but there will likely be a lot of "agree to disagree" resolutions to their conflicts.

They say opposites attract, and that's true. But they can also attack. Depending on various factors, as mentioned earlier, Tom and Marissa might dig in and defend their positions, and their arguments could easily degenerate into bitter battles over who's "right," who's to blame, and what's "wrong" with the other.

I'm not saying that the same thing couldn't happen to the other couple, Hunter and Molly. They certainly won't escape conflict. But their disagreements will tend to be more about "logistical" misunderstandings than fundamental differences over who is "right" or "wrong." While each sees life from their own unique perspective, they have so much in common that they will find themselves agreeing on most everything that matters to them. Their conflicts stand a better chance of being

> I believe the best marriages are the ones in which each partner brings strengths that the other desperately needs.

more like negotiations, with each side trying to find acceptable terms, rather than all-out war bent on mutually assured destruction.

None of us marries the person of our dreams—we marry the person of our imagination. Then we find out who that person really is.

So should people only marry someone who is just like them? By no means! I believe the best marriages are the ones in which each partner brings strengths that the other desperately needs. When two people are very much alike, their limitations are only magnified—to say nothing of the fact that their relationship is likely to be rather tedious (e.g., always boring, or always in crisis).

The trick, of course, is to actually *see* your spouse—to recognize their strengths and see them as strengths, and to allow those strengths to complement yours. Which brings us back to giftedness. If you know your own giftedness, you're in a much better position to help your spouse understand who you are—what you were born to do and do best, what things are "can-dos" for you, and what things you actually can't do. Likewise, the more you can know about your spouse's giftedness, the better positioned you are to honor their strengths, accept their limitations, and adjust your expectations for what it means to love them and live with them.

The apostle Peter, who was a married man, exhorted husbands to "live with your wife in an understanding way" (literally, "according to knowledge").[3] I think of that often in my own marriage. I believe Peter is imploring me to *see* Lynn, to try and crawl inside her skin and see the world as she sees it. Life looks rather different through her eyes than through mine. Not that there's anything wrong with mine. But if all I ever consider is my own outlook, I am being terribly selfish, neglectful, nearsighted (and sometimes blind), controlling, and foolish, all at the same time.

The crazy thing is, you more than likely already *see* your spouse—you just misinterpret what you see! Inborn assets that are actually among your spouse's strengths end up being classified as problems. "My husband's a control freak." "My wife takes an eternity to make a decision! I wish she would just choose!" "There he goes again, chasing another silly idea." "Will she *ever* put that stupid project away and come to bed?"

We're back to judgments and labels. In truth, 90 percent of the people who come my way have been shamed for the very thing that is their real giftedness. And spouses are among the worst at the shame game. It's easy to see why. When you live in a relationship as intimate as marriage, you're going to discover who your spouse really is. And again, because they are different from you, your impulse will be to say, "What's wrong with you?!" That almost always leads to a label.

For every form of giftedness that exists, someone has invented a negative, shame-based label. The person who loves to get things right is called a "perfectionist," or "OCD" (obsessive-compulsive disorder), or "anal retentive." The person who likes to understand things at a deep level is called a "brainiac," or "wonk," or "know-it-all." The person who loves to use their imagination and creativity is called a "dreamer." The person who loves to meet needs and take care of others is called an "enabler." I could go on and on.

In the next chapter I'll talk about the dark side of giftedness. Every form of giftedness creates unintended problems for others, perhaps most especially for one's spouse. But if you focus on the dark side of who your spouse is, you'll end up shaming them as a person, and I guarantee your marriage will suffer.

GIFTEDNESS AND YOUR PARENTING

We live in a culture that says a child is a product. The product begins when you and your spouse make a baby and bring it into the world. From there your task is to give that baby as many advantages as you can in order to help them get a good start in life. At every step of that manufacturing process are countless experts and vendors only too eager to sell you what you need to turn out a fantastic product. Baby-raising is big business!

> Parents don't "make" a person. God makes a person.

At some point your baby leaves the nest, and then you watch to see what sort of product you've turned out. You might even say, "I think we did a pretty good job raising her. She *turned out* okay." Of course, if things don't turn out so well, you'll probably scratch your head and wonder, "Where did we go wrong?"

Regardless of how a child "turns out," where parents go wrong is thinking their child is a product. A child is not a product; a child is a *person.* They're a person designed by God from the womb. Yes, an enormous amount of development takes place, beginning in the womb and continuing throughout infancy and adolescence. But parents don't "make" a person. God makes a person. An infant person, to be sure, but a person nonetheless.

That dramatically changes your role as a parent. Your job is to help that infant person grow into the adult person God intended them to be. The influences of countless other people and systems will contribute to that journey, for better and for worse—other siblings, your extended family, your child's friends and peers, teachers, coaches, tutors, youth workers, the impact of schools, clubs, faith communities, media and all the pieces of the broader culture, and so on. But as the parent, God has given you the assignment of overseeing an infant person's path to adulthood. That's both a privileged and sobering stewardship.

Having raised three daughters, I can testify as an expert witness that child-rearing is even harder than marriage. But a lot of parents make it a lot harder than they need to. They're all worried and busied about doing a lot of things they think will improve the chances of their kid "turning out" all right.

All the while they ignore or slight the most important things, which to my mind boil down to four things: helping their child arrive at adulthood with a relatively healthy emotional life (feeling like they belong, that they matter, that they're loved, that they can trust); having some sort of meaningful relationship with God; having a decent education; and having a good grasp of their core strengths in order to make a contribution to the world and earn a living. If parents only gave their child those four things, that child would have most of what they need to thrive as an adult.

While I care deeply about all four of those projects, my work focuses on the fourth one—helping people understand their core strengths. What can you do as a parent to help your child appreciate their giftedness?

Believe it or not, the most important thing is to start by knowing as much as you can about your own giftedness. That will give you a frame of reference. You'll know more about the phenomenon and how it works in your own experience. Then you can observe it at play in your child's experience. And you certainly don't want to be celebrating your child's giftedness when you don't know what your own is. Sooner or later they're going to ask, "So Daddy, what's your giftedness?" If you don't know, that will signal to your child that giftedness must not really matter very much.

But an even more important reason to know your giftedness is that just as you live out your role as a husband or wife through the lens of your giftedness, you likewise parent according to your giftedness. Your kids instinctively know that whether or not you do.

My girls, for example, knew that if they wanted a plan to come together, they went to their mother. If they wanted to tell jokes and be silly, they came to me. If they wanted to think through a school project, they went to their mother. If they wanted feedback on their writing, they came to me. If they wanted to learn to drive, they went to their mother. If they wanted to prepare a speech, they came to me. (In truth, there were many things the girls preferred to go to their mother for, rather than me. Their mother was infinitely more gifted to the task of parenting than I am.)

So when should you start trying to identify your child's giftedness? The moment they're born. You won't be able to see much. But trust me, it's there. It's very primitive. It has almost no means of expressing itself yet, because the equipment it requires is still too young. So don't get ahead of the child. Just assume it's there and welcome it by letting that little person know how delighted you are about their arrival.

> Observe what gives your child energy, and then feed that energy.

Then you wait and watch. There won't be a lot to see at first, so you may be tempted to lose interest, especially if you're the father. Mothers are blessed with maternal instincts about their children, so they tend to see the signs of personhood a lot sooner.

The key to observing the giftedness of your child is to pay attention to their *energy*. Where do they put their energy? What activities cause them to come alive, to get really interested, to focus on the task? What holds their attention? What activities do they willingly engage in for long periods of time (besides passive activities like watching TV)? Which ones do they want to keep coming back to? Energy in a child is a telltale sign that something is activating their giftedness.

You can't immediately know what that something is. So whatever you do, for about the first twelve years of your child's life, stick with observations of their behavior and stay away from interpretations of it. Otherwise, you're liable to ruin everything!

Just because your six-year-old begs to start piano lessons doesn't mean they have visions of becoming a concert pianist. Their motivation may be to do something their friends are doing. Likewise, when your eighth-grader gives a speech and gets elected class president, that doesn't mean she's predestined for a life in politics. Her giftedness may be about forming relationships, and so she got elected because she was the only nominee that everyone at her school knew.

Giftedness is especially revealed in the mundane.

Never push your child into a path. Rather, see what path seems to be emerging for *them.* Observe what appears to give them energy, and then feed that energy. I call that honoring the gift. You try to work with your child's giftedness, not block it or frustrate it.

That can be hard to do, especially when their giftedness diverges significantly from your own (remember the side-by-side boxes). I see that quite often with a father who is quite successful and whose giftedness exhibits power. He's a goal-oriented, results-driven guy who knows how to set a plan, execute it, and win. Meanwhile, he's got a son who lives in the world of concepts. Today the boy is really into fractals. But a few months later he's spending all his time exploring the acoustics of musical instruments. However, that peters out when he discovers chess. And so it goes. Whatever the boy does, he does so with a passion. But his passions keep changing.

Now you can imagine how frustrated his father must be. He keeps urging his son to set goals. "You're never going to get anywhere without a goal and a plan," he tells him. But guess what? The young man is not trying to "get" anywhere! That's not in his motivational makeup. He's on an intellectual odyssey, exploring what to him seems like an endlessly fascinating world. There is no destination. There's only the journey. The father will only ruin him if he tries to force him to get his act together and conform to the father's idea of what matters in life (which is driven by the father's giftedness).

So what if no apparent "path" seems to be emerging for your child?

Then as the parent, expand the universe of possibilities. Give your child exposure to as many different kinds of activities, experiences, and circumstances as possible.

As they go through those moments, pay attention to their energy. Just see how they respond. Even situations that you think are inconsequential, like your family picking up your spouse at the airport, or routine, like making dinner, or even terrible like the death of a family member, may reveal important clues about your child's giftedness. Indeed, giftedness is especially revealed in the mundane, and also in what your child does when *they* get to choose the activity. As my colleagues and I like to say, when it comes to spotting giftedness, everything is evidence.

One way to capture your observations is to keep a simple journal on your child. You can write an entry whenever you notice something interesting, along the lines of "Today my child participated in a play at school and totally loved it. She said she especially liked it when everyone laughed after she presented her line." Or, "Today my child had a flute recital. She didn't practice for it the way she was supposed to, but when it came time to perform, she knocked it out of the park. I was simply amazed." Or, "I can't get my child to put down the book he started reading yesterday on the Civil War. He's just absorbed in it!"

If you collect those kinds of entries over several years, you'll end up with a considerable body of data from which to start drawing some conclusions about your child's giftedness. You'll start to see some themes and patterns repeating themselves. Then you'll be in a better position to help your child start becoming aware of and owning their strengths and interests.

You can also keep a portfolio of your child's accomplishments, especially the ones that they, by their own admission, really enjoyed and are really proud of. That collection could include things they've made, stories or papers they've written, mementos of various adventures they've had or achievements they treasure, and especially photos, videos, and/or audio recordings of them doing their "thing" or describing some event they found especially exciting.

To be honest, I'm not sure that helping your child wake up to their giftedness takes a whole lot more than that. It's about observing first, then over time beginning to recognize some recurring themes and behaviors, then pointing out those themes to your child and affirming them as valuable assets, and then celebrating your child's accomplishments when *they* feel they've done well. (By the way, it does no good—in fact, it's harmful—to tell your child that everything they do is amazing, fantastic, the best ever. Let *them* tell you what they find meaningful and satisfying.)

An ancient proverb often prescribed to parents as child-rearing wisdom states, "Train up a child in the way he should go . . . Even when he is old he will not depart from it."[4] The words "train up" derive from the idea of stimulating a palate for, creating a taste for, developing a desire for. The words "in the way he should go" refer to the God-given bent of the child, their natural disposition, the "way" God has made them.

In short, this proverb commands parents to pay attention to their child's giftedness and help them embrace it, own it, and become a master at using it. I can't imagine a higher privilege—to receive a tiny little person who is actually a gift of God to the world, and then to slowly, carefully, but very intentionally supervise the unwrapping of that gift so that they can carry out the "good works" that have been prepared from eternity for them to do.

GIFTEDNESS AND YOUR COWORKERS

Everything I've said so far in this chapter applies to the ways you interact with everyone where you work. Once again, the more you know about giftedness, and especially about your own giftedness, the better you'll be able to relate to your coworkers and to help them relate to you.

The vast majority of work takes place through teams. If you work on a team, by now you can see that everyone on your team has their own unique giftedness, which affects (a) their job fit and (b) their relationships with everyone else on the team. It doesn't matter whether everyone on your team has the same occupation (engineers, nurses, surveyors, counselors, accountants, cops, etc.). Everyone comes to their job with a unique form of giftedness, and all of that giftedness interacts like so:

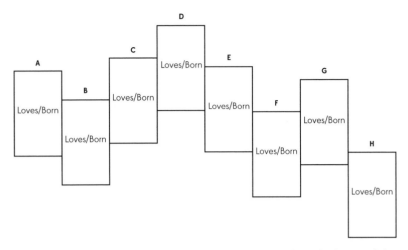

When I work with teams, we actually lay out the giftedness of the whole team like that, side by side. Seeing a team that way has numerous advantages. It gives you insight into the relationships members have with one another. It shows you what your collective strengths are, and where they reside. It shows you what gifts you may need but are missing. Most importantly, it helps everyone *see* everyone else.

I think of teams and organizations like toolboxes. In a toolbox you have lots of different tools. Each of them is designed to accomplish a particular task really well. But most jobs require more than one tool. In fact, the more complex the task, the more tools are required. So the question any team leader needs to ask is: Do we have the right tools for what we're trying to accomplish, and are we using the tools in the proper way?

The power of having the right tools and using them the right way is almost beyond imagining. But then, that's the trick, isn't it? Someone has to align all that giftedness. Otherwise it ends up defeating itself, because people waste their energy fighting and/or working around each other instead of focusing their efforts on the larger task.

Enter the manager. It's the manager's job to get the energy of the team working in concert. There's a lot I could say to managers, but I want to stay focused on you and on the relationship you have with whoever manages you.

The number one reason people quit their job is because they can't stand their boss. Conversely, one of the most important "sticky" factors that can attract and hold someone to a job is having a boss they admire, respect, and trust. That manager-report relationship is essential to harmony and effectiveness in the workplace.

Your job-fit radically affects your relationship to your boss. Look at the two situations below. Which employee do you suppose will have the most trouble with their boss?

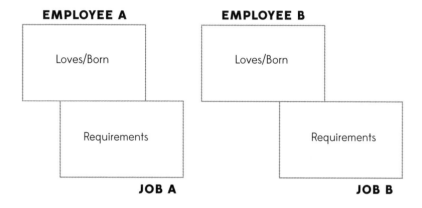

EMPLOYEE A

Loves/Born

Requirements

JOB A

EMPLOYEE B

Loves/Born

Requirements

JOB B

Obviously it's Employee B. Employee A is in a good job-fit. When you've got great fit, you tend to do great work. Needless to say, your boss is going to like that, and so your conflicts will likely be minimal. But if you're in a poor job-fit like Employee B, you'll tend to do the job poorly. You'll drop balls. You'll make mistakes. You'll do things halfway. You'll find a lot to complain about. And your boss will probably be tearing their hair out with frustration—and you can bet you're going to hear about it. A lot! Conflict with your boss will skyrocket.

That's the job-fit. There's also the relational fit—your giftedness side by side with your boss's giftedness. The scenario here is similar to what we saw above in the two married couples, Hunter and Molly, and Tom and Marissa:

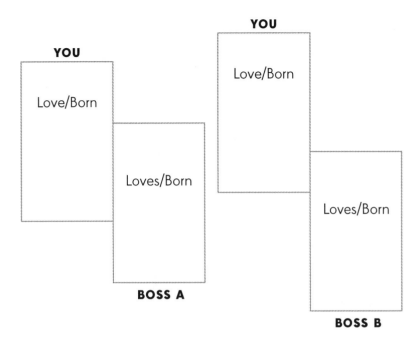

You're naturally going to get along better with Boss A than with Boss B, because you and Boss A see things a lot alike. You may be very similar in terms of what motivates you, or you may have very complementary strengths that allow you to benefit and reinforce each other. But your relationship with Boss B is going to take a lot of work on both sides. You literally see the world differently, and what matters to you is not at all what matters to your boss, and vice versa. In short, your potential for conflict with Boss B is high because it takes so much "can-do" for the two of you to relate to one another.

What management style works for you? That's critical in how you get along with your boss. *Everyone* needs some form of management, but everyone prefers to be managed a bit differently. Some people need more direction from their boss than others. Some prefer specific kinds of input. Here are a few examples:

HOW DO YOU NEED TO BE MANAGED?

"HELP ME GET STARTED"

Set me up for success by explaining everything clearly, training me properly, pointing out the likely risks and problems, and preparing me to do the work. Then I can take it from there.

"BE THERE WHEN I NEED YOU"

I'll work at my job, but don't run off and leave me. I'd prefer if you check up on me periodically and let me know how I'm doing. That gives me confidence that I'm on track and meeting your expectations.

"TELL ME WHAT TO DO"

I'm going to wait to act until I know exactly what you want me to do, and how. I don't want to do the wrong thing, and I don't want to do it the wrong way. You're the boss!

"LET'S DO IT TOGETHER"

I know you're over me on the organizational chart, but let's work as peers to get things done. You give me your input on what I'm doing.

"LEAVE ME ALONE!"

Tell me what you want me to do, then I'll go do it. I'll check in with you as needed to report in and get input. Otherwise, please don't interfere.

"COACH ME"

I know I have unique talents, but I want you to make me better. Watch me in action, give me feedback, critique my performance, kick me in the rear end when I need it, and tell me you believe in me.

How do you prefer to be managed? Have you ever thought about that? If you're not getting the management you require, you won't do your job as well, or you'll resent your boss, or both. For example, suppose you need lots of up-front orientation to what you're supposed to do ("Help Me Get Started"). But your boss just hands you an assignment and throws you in over your head. You're going to feel uneasy moving forward. Conversely, if you prefer to work fairly independently ("Leave Me Alone!"), but your boss keeps phoning you every twenty minutes to see how it's going, you're going to feel very irritated.

So what do you do if your supervisor isn't providing the kind of supervision you need? Well, you don't have to suffer in silence. Speak up about it! Have a meeting with your boss to explain what your needs are. Be professional, but be clear. Talk about *you*: "I'm a person who really needs a lot of input from my supervisor" or, "I feel like I do my best when you let me completely finish an assignment, and then we debrief." Don't make it about your boss: "You're always nagging me," or, "You got me started but then sort of ran off on me."

As you consider how to address a supervisory issue, keep in mind that every boss has a unique style in the way they manage. Some of those styles parallel the descriptions shown above: "I'll help you get started"; "I'll be there if you need me"; "Let me tell you what to do"; "We're going to do this together"; "Here's what I want, now it's up to you"; "Let me give you some feedback." You can't change the way your manager manages people. But it at least helps to recognize how they see their role and then accommodate yourself as best as possible to satisfying their expectations.

Of course, one final reality also needs to be pointed out: a lot of people in management roles have no fundamental giftedness for managing others. They weren't born to that task. As a result, they have no inherent strengths for that task, nor any real motivation to do it. Regardless, they've been placed in a supervisory role. I think businesses are utterly stupid to do that, but it happens everywhere.

You may have a boss like that (or someday will). If so, remind yourself that they are in a poor job-fit, at least as far as the management part of their job. They're "managing" out of can-do, not born-to-do. That's a shame. But a bad job-fit does not make a bad person. So rather than write off your boss as a jerk, an idiot, a control freak, a psycho, or any of the countless other labels that circulate in workplaces, *see* them as a person. They're in a mismatch doing the best they can, which may be awful. Is there anything you can do that would help them and help their relationship with you go better?

GIFTEDNESS AND YOUR AGING PARENTS

My father passed away recently, so it's especially poignant to me to note that giftedness has some profound and far-reaching implications for how things end up between you and your aging parents.

The relationship with an elderly parent becomes a lot more challenging as they move toward the end of their life. They may have health issues that you have to attend to. There's the whole question of where they're going to live and what care they're going to require. They can become a lot harder to communicate with if they grow hard of hearing. If they develop something like dementia or Alzheimer's, their very personhood may slowly slip into the shadows. And then, of course, there's all the housekeeping stuff like wills, and inheritance, and health care directives, and burial preferences.

Overriding all of these matters is the lifelong relationship you've had with your parent, whether great, or just good, or not so good, or terrible, or even nonexistent. That way of relating still dramatically affects everything, except that the roles start reversing and you gradually become the one who must exercise responsibility and look after your parent. That's complicated!

In the midst of it all, it's very common to feel an instinctive impulse to try and "connect" with one's parent before they die. Not always; some child-parent relationships are irretrievably broken, a terribly sad reality that yields nothing but pain and trouble for both sides. But in the main, children at least have a desire to say some things and to hear some things before their parent is no longer with them.

> I found that the process of discovering my dad's giftedness turned out to be transformational in my relationship with him.

In my own case, I found that the process of discovering my dad's giftedness turned out to be transformational in my relationship with him. I believe the same could hold true for most anyone. Remember that the best way to identify someone's giftedness is through their stories, particularly their stories of meaningful achievement (see chapter 5). So I'm encouraging you to rediscover your aging parents by asking them to tell you some of their stories.

There's a section in the back of the book that offers a formal process for doing that. But you don't necessarily have to follow that approach. You can just sit down with mom or dad on some rainy afternoon and ask them to tell you about growing up. What activities did they most enjoy doing? How did they spend their time? How did they while away their hours as a kid? Most elderly people have a lot of time on their hands. So your parent will likely be more than happy to talk about things they've done in life that they enjoyed doing and feel they did well. After all, you're asking them to talk about the best moments of their life!

Perhaps you feel you already know all that. Maybe so. I certainly heard my dad tell numerous stories that I'd heard a hundred times. But this time I was listening with different ears. This time I was trying to *see* the person.

That's something I don't think a lot of children do, at least not until later in life, if ever. They keep seeing their parent as their parent—and relating to them on that basis. But going on an intentional search to find out your parent's giftedness will lead you to an amazing discovery: it turns out that your parent is a person, just as you are. They've had to contend with the same challenges of life you contend with. Knowing their giftedness can give you a lot of insight, understanding, and perhaps for the first time, empathy and compassion, for how they lived their life—as a person, not just a parent.

Remember what I said earlier about giftedness and the way you parent? Well, the same dynamics applied to the way your parent parented you. They did so through the lens of their giftedness. Maybe that approach was helpful, maybe it proved harmful. But at least recognize that that's all they knew to do—just like you're doing with your kids.

If you've always had real challenges relating to your parent, *seeing* them as a person can go a long way toward healing hurtful memories and improving the relationship. If nothing else, it may temper the way you ask that instinctive question, "What's *wrong* with you?!" Maybe there's nothing "wrong" with your parent, and never has been. They just happen to be rather different than you.

GIFTEDNESS AND YOUR DARK SIDE

Giftedness is what I call "dangerous knowledge."

When I was in high school, I took calculus, chemistry, and biology. I made straight As in each of them. However, if you asked me today what the specific gravity of water is, or what a quadratic equation is, I couldn't tell you if my life depended on it. Yes, I took those classes and studied hard and learned the material. But as soon as I got the final grade, that knowledge quickly started leaking out of my brain. That was not dangerous knowledge.

Dangerous knowledge is knowledge you *never* forget. It's like a one-way door where, once you pass through it, your life will never be the same. Dangerous knowledge is when you come home from work and your wife says, "Guess what, honey, we're pregnant!" Dangerous knowledge is when your doctor points to an X-ray and says, "See that spot? That's cancer."

Giftedness is a form of dangerous knowledge. If you make the effort to actually look in the mirror to discover your giftedness, you'll never quite forget what you see. Nor would I want you to forget. I want you to use your giftedness to make a real contribution in the world.

But that points to another sense in which giftedness is "dangerous": it involves actual power. Your gift is a tool, not a toy. It arms you with a means of accomplishing something and having real effect on the world and people. That's great if what you do yields worthy results. But what if you use your giftedness in ways that are harmful?

Every form of giftedness has a potential dark side. The gift itself is inherently good, but morally neutral. It can be used for good or ill. In this chapter I want to talk about the potential for your giftedness to go wrong.

UNINTENDED CONSEQUENCES

Without even trying, your giftedness can create problems for yourself and other people. Are you aware of that?

A lifelong friend of mine is a born musician. When I was growing up, I thought he was the best guitarist in the world (I later learned that Jimi Hendrix and Stevie Ray Vaughan were just a notch or two better—but honestly, not by much). This guy was exceptionally creative. He could write lyrics on the level of a James Taylor or John Lennon. And I'm glad to say that he followed his giftedness and became a professional musician. While he never got "discovered" or became famous, he nonetheless has had a productive career writing and producing music.

So that's all good. But it was not in his nature to remember appointments. He'd agree to get together and the rest of us would show up at the appointed hour. But not him. Sometimes he'd come terribly late—I mean, like an hour or more late. And sometimes he didn't show at all. So of course, we'd ask him what happened. "Oh, wow, man, I'm sorry," he'd say. "I met this guy who's selling a mandolin, so I had to talk with him." Or, "I forgot my mom needed me to go pick up my brother." Or, "I thought we were meeting on Thursday, but yeah, I guess we did say Tuesday. Sorry, man." That scenario became so predictable it was laughable.

Now so far in this book, I've gone easy on how we should respond to someone like that. Instead of writing them off, or shaming them, or giving them a piece of our mind, we need to recognize as best we can how they're wired, and then accept the limitations of that and deal with the challenges it creates for us. I still believe that.

But here I want to turn the focus the other way—actually, on you, because you're just like my friend. No, you don't necessarily space out on remembering appointments. But there's inevitably something you do, just by virtue of how you're naturally wired, that irritates other people or affects them negatively.

For example, are you a visionary who is brilliant at casting vision and getting people to buy in? You might be surprised at how many people have been disappointed because expectations you've created haven't turned out quite the way you sold them.

Or maybe you have a gift for analysis. You can point out the flaws in a line of reasoning like nobody's business. But are you aware that your adolescent daughter remains silent about what matters most to her because she doesn't want a critique, just someone to listen?

> You create problems for the people around you, just by being you.

Or say you have a profound sensitivity to meeting needs, which gifts you supremely to the task of mothering. But have you ever considered that your children may be becoming so dependent on you that they cannot function on their own?

Every form of giftedness creates unintended consequences for other people. And we can see that everywhere. Celebrities create problems for their families. Executives create problems for their assistants and lieutenants. Surgeons create problems for nurses. Nurses create problems for patients. Secretaries create problems for their bosses. Teachers create problems for their principals. Athletes create problems for their coaches. Even Mother Teresa created problems for her sisters at the Missionaries of Charity.

You likewise create problems for the people around you. Just by being you.

Not that you intend to! Let me be quick to state that. By no means do you intentionally try to make trouble for someone else. In fact, most of the time, you're not even aware you're doing so. That's why it's called it an *unintended* consequence.

So should you just give up and not use your gift? Of course not! That's not even possible. The unintended consequences of you being you are unavoidable.

The better path is to become mature in the exercise of your gift. That starts by recognizing how that gift might create problems for others. That takes us back to the side-by-side boxes in the previous chapter. If you can try to *see* the other people around you through the lens of their giftedness, you'll gain an appreciation for how your gift might affect theirs.

And of course you can always ask them directly. In fact, lots of times they'll come to you first. They may be mad, or upset, or confused, or sad, or shaming, Which doesn't feel very good. Nobody likes to be attacked. But I might suggest you listen carefully to *what* they are saying (or trying to say), regardless of *how* they are saying it, and consider: "What is my part in this? Is there something I'm instinctively doing that is creating some real problems for this person?" If so, you can acknowledge their feelings, apologize for causing trouble, and then figure out how to handle these issues in the future.

Unfortunately, one thing you can never do is eliminate the unintended consequences of being yourself.

THE BURDEN OF YOUR GIFT

Giftedness is about motivational energy. When you're operating in your sweet spot, you put your heart into the task. You care about it.

When I make my bed in the morning, I don't put my heart into making it. In fact, I'm usually thinking about something else. But put me in front of someone trying to figure what to do with their life. Now it's game on for Bill! Now I'm all focus. I'm totally engaged. Now it counts.

That power of giftedness to summon the best of one's energies is what fuels the great accomplishments of the world. When people put their heart and soul into what they're doing, incredible things can happen.

But there's an inherent danger in that bargain. The very fact that you give your heart to a task means your heart is going to be affected in the doing of that task. You will react emotionally to what happens—good and bad.

When the builder who loves to construct new projects steps back and sees his finished product in all its glory, he feels great! When the accountant whose giftedness drives her to get things right sees her financial plan succeeding on the spreadsheets, she smiles (accountants don't pump their fists in the air the way the rest of us do). When the firefighter who thrives on the thrill and challenge of a crisis carries the child to safety from the burning home, he knows in his heart he's done a good job.

But what about the reactions that don't feel so good? That builder who delights in the finished product knows that with a little more time and a slightly larger budget, he could have turned out a masterpiece instead of the humble structure the customer could afford. He may feel a little sad about that. Likewise, that accountant who is happy that her plan is succeeding nonetheless worries about all the things outside of her control that could dash that plan to pieces. And the fireman goes home at dawn grateful that he saved a life. But he lies awake thinking about the mother who didn't make it out, and wonders if there was anything else he could have done.

Every form of giftedness comes with what I call "the burden of the gift" attached to it. The gift extracts an emotional toll on the person simply by virtue of them being who they are. And there's no way around that.

The burden means a creative type has high highs and low lows. Someone with a mind for maximizing capital feels intense irritation with those who waste their time. Someone who excels at building relationships feels hurt when someone they care about has a moral failure. A person who loves to understand things in depth feels insulted when others want to reduce things to simplistic answers. An individual who is motivated to meet needs through social work or teaching in the inner city gets burned out, overwhelmed by all the needs around them. Meanwhile, a surgeon, a pilot, a police officer, or someone else trained to stay cool under pressure wakes up to the chilling reality that they have lost the ability to feel.

Whatever your giftedness is, it will have an emotional burden attached to it. The only way to escape that burden would be to become someone else. But of course then you'd have to contend with the burden of having that person's giftedness. Better the devil you know than the one you don't know!

Is there a particular emotional state that frequently recurs for you? I suggest you consider how those feelings may actually be linked to your giftedness.

But what is the remedy for the burden of the gift? The only remedy I'm aware of is the intentional practice of forcing your gift to rest.

In the Old Testament we're given the idea of Sabbath, which means to rest. Most people think of the Sabbath as a day off—Saturday if you're Jewish, Sunday if you're Christian. Except that knowledge work has completely turned the notion of a day off on its head. In fact, I think those of us who are knowledge workers need to seriously revisit what we mean by the Sabbath if we have any hope of mitigating the burden of our gifts.

> We're discovering that 24/7 access is dangerously unhealthy.

The command to work six days and refrain from work on the seventh makes perfect sense in an agrarian economy. People in that world lived according to the natural rhythms of day and night, the cycles of the moon, the four seasons, and so forth. But today's knowledge workers work in their minds, not on the land. On top of that, electricity has eliminated the darkness of night and the effects of seasonal weather, and communications technologies have eliminated distance. The result is that knowledge workers are "on" or potentially "on," anytime, anywhere.

The luxury of being constantly wired is a convenience—until it's inconvenient. If you've ever had your vacation interrupted by a crisis text from the office, you know what I'm talking about. In fact, we're discovering that 24/7 access is actually dangerously unhealthy. We never rest. As a result, some of us are no longer focusing. A lot of younger people in our culture are even in danger of losing the ability to focus. Or else they're becoming hyperfocused, and thus unable to function.

A Sunday morning church service, followed by a day of watching football games and catching up on emails and Facebook doesn't even begin to rest your gift.

I don't have room to go into this problem in detail, but I will say this. Sabbath, or rest, is not a quaint custom of a bygone era that is slowly fading from the stage. Yes, society may be gradually setting aside the rituals and customs associated with Sabbath. But Sabbath was never about a custom or a day but about a reality built into the fabric of the world and the nature of human beings. We were designed to work, and to that end we were each given a gift. But we were not made to work all the time. At some point and in some way, we're supposed to rest, which means letting our gift rest.

It may be that the only way of doing that is to take the radical—and for some, unthinkable—step of unplugging from the grid for a period of time and doing something completely *unproductive*, yet genuinely refreshing. You may have to experiment a bit to learn what it takes for you to enforce Sabbath on yourself. And you certainly have to be careful about "unplugging" in ways that leave others in the lurch without you (e.g., your team at work). But it simply won't happen if you're not intentional.

THE POTENTIAL FOR EVIL

The worst sins that people commit are not the result of their so-called weaknesses but rather of using their God-given strengths for selfish, sinful, and evil purposes. Hitler, the Nazis, and the Germans of the 1930s and '40s had a great deal of giftedness on their side. The international drug trade has not grown to 1 percent of all global trade without a lot of people's giftedness in play. As with the good works, so with the bad: nothing of consequence happens in the world apart from people gifted to the task.

So what's the possibility you could end up devoting the best of your energies to the worst of ends? A lot greater than you probably think. The danger lies in overestimating yourself while underestimating the nature and power of evil.

I suppose because my middle name is David, I've always felt an affinity for King David in the Old Testament. I've spent a lot of time reflecting on that incredible man, about whom we have so much information in Scripture. One of the questions everyone asks about David is how he could commit adultery with Bathsheba and have her husband murdered to try and cover up his indiscretion. I think a lot of the answer lies in his giftedness.

It's not too difficult to figure out what David's giftedness was. The evidence from the text is pretty overwhelming.[1] As a boy he watches sheep. Occasionally that requires taking on a wild animal, like a lion or a bear. His first big event is the contest with Goliath, whom he kills. Afterward he becomes Saul's armor-bearer and is set over the men of war. That takes him into numerous battles, where he succeeds so brilliantly that the women sing, "Saul has slain his thousands, and David his ten thousands!"

From there we find David in one bloody encounter after another. On one occasion the Bible says he slaughtered a band of raiders "from the twilight until the evening of the next day." When he defeats the Moabites, he has the survivors separated into three lines, two of which he puts to death. When he takes the city of Rabbah, he condemns the survivors to execution by means of saws, sharp instruments, axes, and a brick kiln.

> A warrior is instinctively wired to use force. One potential dark side of that gift is murder.

Whatever else we can say about David, he clearly was a man built for battle. To put it crassly, he was a killing machine. He was, as the Lord states, a "man of war."[2] He was a warrior. Indeed, he was a champion. Israel needed a king to crush its enemies and consolidate the nation. David was the perfect man for the job.

Now that may shed some light on the puzzling verses near the end of Psalm 139, which seem so out of place: "O that You would slay the wicked, O God . . . Depart from me, therefore, men of bloodshed. . . ."

I'll leave it to the commentators to explain all the theological and ethical questions this passage raises. I would simply observe that the expression of violent hatred for the Lord's enemies is what you'd expect from a man who was made for war.

But another thing we know about David is that he genuinely sought after God. So Psalm 139 ends with a rather poignant prayer for personal integrity: "Search me, O God, and know my heart; / Try me and know my anxious thoughts; / And see if there be any hurtful way in me, / And lead me in the everlasting way." David wants to be acceptable to God. He wants whatever bad stuff is in his heart to be brought to light.

I believe God took him up on that prayer—and He used the affair with Bathsheba to do so. It's as if God said to David, "Okay, you really want to know what's in your heart? Let me show you. You're a man of war, and I've ordained you to be a great champion for My people. But your strength for fighting is not a gift when your heart is not aligned with Mine. The hurtful way in you is that you'll turn to that very gift when you find yourself in a fix and end up acting just like the wicked you despise."

And that's exactly what happens when David capriciously ravishes

Uriah's wife, then has him killed when an unwanted pregnancy threatens to expose him. A warrior is instinctively wired to use force. One potential dark side of that gift is murder.

Confronted by the prophet Nathan, David outs with an admission of his guilt. Then he composes Psalm 51. If you read that psalm, you'll find echoes of Psalm 139, and indeed of David's whole life, reverberating through his chastened mind. "Search me" and "try me" become "wash me" and "cleanse me." "I am fearfully and wonderfully made" becomes "I was brought forth in iniquity / And in sin my mother conceived me." "Depart from me...men of bloodshed" becomes "deliver me from bloodguiltiness." In Psalm 139, David wants to slay the wicked. In Psalm 51, he sees that he himself is among the wicked.

The lesson is: be careful what you pray for! But perhaps even more careful about what you're not praying for. David didn't know what he didn't know until he prayed to find out. Then God showed him his dark side.

Now let me tell you about me.

When I was in junior high school, I was a ringleader in a blatant case of bullying. When those in charge found out about it, I was summoned to the principal's office and appropriately confronted, rebuked, punished, and warned of the consequences of future offenses. Once I realized what I had done, I was remorseful and deeply ashamed. I feel shame even now in writing about that incident, especially as I look back on it from an adult perspective and realize all of its ramifications.

The fuel of evil is desire.

At the time I was afraid of being kicked out of school. But when I grew older, I realized that the scariest thing about that behavior was how good it felt. I had actually enjoyed teasing and dominating another person. It was, in its own perverse and disgusting way, fun. You see, that activity fit with my giftedness. A twisted fit, to be sure, but a fit nonetheless.

In fact, when I later went back and reviewed some of the times in my life when I was at my worst, I discovered that that act of bullying was by no means an isolated incident. I discovered numerous other acts of aggression and domination elsewhere in my young life. And here's what's chilling: many of them occurred when I was in the sweet spot of using my giftedness and actually being praised for my behavior!

By sheer grace a rather imposing adult intervened at a key moment and gave me an offer I couldn't refuse to put an end to my bullying. Thank God I heeded his correction! But what might have happened to me if someone like that had never showed up? How much evil could Bill as an adult bully have inflicted on the world?

At the time, people would have said (and did say), "You know, Bill is a really 'good' kid." Most all of my friends who participated in that incident were "good" kids. Everyone I knew at school was a "good" kid. And we all grew up to be "good" people. Most everyone you meet seems to be a "good" person. But somewhere inside every one of us are tiny cells of mutated desire and satisfaction—"motivational cancers."

What do you suppose those motivational cancers could be for you? Perhaps the smirking satisfaction of getting away with something you know is wrong? Or the congratulatory feeling of outsmarting someone through a deception or fraud? Or the feeling of power you get by breaking a law you think is "stupid"? Or the smugness you feel in ignoring a parking ticket? Or the pleasure of lust?

> Little do we consider the unseen devils that read our desires and exploit them to our peril.

We'll talk about the source of evil in a moment, but the fuel of evil is desire. When an activity feels good, we want to do it again. Giftedness, too, is fueled by desire—what we love to do and are born to do. Giftedness is thus the perfect host for evil.

All you need once you get started is time. Time is the leaky faucet of development. A drop or two is nothing. But a steady drip, drip, drip over time grows into a flood. Remember the ten thousand-hour principle? Spend ten thousand hours playing a violin and you'll end up at the world-class level. So what happens to someone who devotes their energy to ten thousand hours of fraud or theft or deceit or lust or bullying?

Giftedness is all about desire—which should caution us to carefully examine what makes us feel good. Remember, the giftedness itself is not the problem. What the giftedness serves determines everything (see the next chapter).

Which brings us to the question of where evil comes from in the first place. One narrative in our culture says that evil doesn't really exist and that most people are basically good. To my mind, that seems like an egregious case of denial and looking the other way. All the evidence, which seems abundant, incontrovertible, and mounting by the day, the year, and the century, points to something terribly wrong with the world, and to humans as the primary wrongdoers.

Another narrative says that evil stems from physiochemical processes gone bad in one's brain. That and bad parenting. I can buy that in cases like a mentally ill person who breaks with reality and shoots up a campus, or a teen who commits some horrible crime after having been brutally tortured for most of her young life. But that doesn't explain a Tim McVeigh or a Khalid Sheikh Mohammed or a Bernie Madoff. Rogues like that may have ended up in madness, but they didn't start there. What turns someone to the dark side?

Well, just as I have found that what the Bible says about God designing humans is true, I find that what it says about evil is also true. Evil is not an idea or a philosophical category but a real enemy engaged in an actual battle against God over human beings. We are the prize. Created with the faculty of choice, each of us has the freedom to let evil win in our life. I think C. S. Lewis got it right in *The Screwtape Letters*, where he described how we humans think we are so strong and independent, and we get so focused on our project of making a living and doing as we please. Little do we consider the unseen devils that read our desires and exploit them to our peril.

Your giftedness is dangerous because it's real power, and that power is corruptible. It can do real harm. Not because it gets out of control but precisely because it becomes very much under control—under the control of evil. At some point you begin to *intentionally* use it for a dark purpose. In fact, you can get better and better at that purpose over time. You can even turn it into a lifestyle.

Now reinforce that habit by justifying it with a set of deeply held attitudes and convictions, an overarching ideology, and all the interlocking systems and rituals of culture. Team it up with like-minded people who bring the power of their gifts alongside. Orchestrate everyone into a collective cause and a mindset of madness. In the fullness of time, set the match of opportunity to it all. The world will be shocked at the blaze.

For any one of us, the potential for evil is beyond what we imagine. That's why we can never pay enough attention to what—or whom—our giftedness serves. Serve yourself and you'll discover that you're really serving something else altogether, something dark and devious and devilish. But of course, the potential of doing good is also beyond our wildest dreams. In the final chapter, I'll talk about the path that I believe brings those dreams into reality.

GIFTEDNESS AND YOUR CALLING

"It's not about you." So begins Rick Warren's mega-bestseller, *The Purpose-Driven Life*. That has to be one the best first sentences of a book since Genesis 1:1.

"It's not about you." I couldn't agree more. So much wisdom wrapped up in those four simple words. So many implications. So appropriate for our times. And so true.

But incurably contrarian as I am, I want to make one quarter-twist to that assertion: it's not about you—until it *is* about you! Then it seems like it's all about you.

The questions of purpose are all about you: Who am I? Why am I here? What should I do with my life? What should I be doing for work? Do I matter? Am I making any difference in the world? What are my strengths? What's my calling? What am I passionate about? What do I have to offer? Am I good enough? Am I capable enough? Do I have what it takes? Am I worthy? Is there any hope for me?

Rick Warren does a much better job than I can explaining that this world is ultimately not about you but about God. But in this book, my focus *is* on you. And if it's about you, it's about God, too. The two of you are inseparably linked together, the way an artistic masterpiece is linked to a master artist. That's how God set it all up. Whatever involves you involves Him.

WHOSE LIFE IS IT, ANYWAY?

The prevailing story in our culture says that your life is your own. You have to take responsibility for yourself. You are the master of your fate. What you do with your life is totally up to you. We even have laws in place to protect everyone's right to self-determination.

Unfortunately, giftedness presents that way of thinking with an inconvenient truth: your life is a gift, not something you sovereignly own outright.

No one wants to hear that! "What do you mean, my life is not my own? That's ridiculous! That sounds totally oppressive and enslaving. I won't stand for that!"

No one wants to be owned. The people of Jesus' day certainly didn't. They despised the Romans who occupied their land. One imposition they especially resented was a poll tax they were forced to pay. Jesus' enemies tried to exploit that conflict by posing Him with a trick question: Under God's law, was it right for the Jews to pay the tax to their pagan overlords? If Jesus said yes, He would not be a good Jew. If He said no, He would be liable for treason.

Jesus asked for one of the coins used to pay the tax. Pointing to it, He asked, "This engraving—who does it look like? And whose name is on it?" His opponents confirmed that the coin had been issued by Caesar. To which Jesus replied, "Then give Caesar what is his."

In one simple object lesson, Jesus sidestepped their trap by posing the overriding issues of ownership and authority. Like it or not, the Romans were in charge. Paying the tax meant acknowledging that reality, not necessarily agreeing with it.

But then, as He so often did, Jesus turned the tables on His enemies by adding a parting shot: "and give God what is his."[1]

What in the world is that about? Well, given the context, it's clearly about ownership and authority. Jesus is saying, if you give Caesar what belongs to him, why not give God what belongs to Him? After all, He's in charge of everything and everyone. He owns it all.

Including you.

What do we see when we look at you? Who do you look like? And whose name, or inscription, is on you? God's! Because that's what it means for you to be made in God's image. Every time someone looks at you, whether they realize it or not—whether *you* realize it or not—they're seeing a unique expression of God that they otherwise wouldn't get to see. God has stamped you with His image, His likeness. When we deal with you, it turns out we're dealing with God, too. He made you to remind people of Him. He owns you.

> Anytime our gift is decoupled from the Gift-giver, things will not end well.

Except that God is not in any way like the capricious and authoritarian Caesars. What He owns He delights in and broods over like a mother hen.

And yet the human heart instinctively resists submitting to a higher authority, whether it be God or anyone else. We all want to be our own kings and queens. Which is actually further evidence that we are stamped with God's image: we instinctively incline toward ruling.

You can see that this puts you in a bit of a bind. A crisis, actually. At some point while you're trying to answer the questions of life, you're going to have to decide who owns you and who's in charge—you, or God? Is it "My will be done" or "Thy will be done"? That's the question that underlies all other questions.

HAVING IT YOUR WAY

Call me cynical, but I can't imagine that most people will choose to say, "Thy will be done." At least, not in the individualistic culture in which I live. Can you? Look at the people around you. What do you see? I see a lot of folks rejecting that arrangement outright: "No way!" A lot more have adopted a rather dismissive attitude about it all: "Maybe God owns me, maybe not. But so what?"

I see a lot of others who've decided to hedge their bets. In their heart they know God is real, so they can't just blow Him off. But they're certainly not prepared to hand over the deed to their life. Who knows where that might lead! So they try to steer a middle course and adopt a lifestyle of largely doing life their way, but tolerating "a little bit of God" on the side. You know, some church attendance, maybe occasional prayers before a meal or something, having a preacher at weddings and funerals, that sort of thing. God has His place in the picture, but He's in the background—often way in the background. He's certainly not in charge.

And then there's a bunch of people who for some reason think they can strike a deal with God: "Lord, I'll try to be a good person and not do anything too bad, and in exchange You bless me with good health, a decent income, and happiness." They turn God into a celestial credit card. It's okay to max it out, just don't get behind in the payments. But it's still all about them.

And finally, I see an awful lot of procrastinators who simply put the question off by saying, "I'll get to all of this stuff someday. Right now I've got other fish to fry."

No one wants to be owned, including me. But nevertheless, a primary law of human nature remains in effect: anytime our gift is decoupled from the Gift-giver, things will not end well.

Even if they appeared to start off well. That's been the case for me and 76 million other Baby Boomers (perhaps you're one of them). When we were graduating from college, the United States was the only game in town, economically speaking. Europe was still rebuilding from World War II. The Soviet Union was starting to gasp under the weight of the socialist, bureaucratic bloat that would ultimately be its undoing. China was still under Mao. India, Japan, and the other Asian players were still on their way up. South America and Africa were not even in consideration.

And so there were plenty of jobs for us. So many, in fact, that you could jump around all through your twenties and try things out, with very few consequences. You didn't have to get serious about life until thirty or later. But by then, most Boomers had settled into a decent-paying job that covered a mortgage. From there, the money started to flow.

There's nothing wrong with a strong economy. But it was all about us. Favored, gifted, educated, with nothing standing in our way, the world was our oyster. "My will be done" became our credo. And in no time at all, the Me Generation, which swore it would never repeat the sins of its parents by engaging in those awful vices of greed and materialism, grew up to become the most affluent, self-involved, self-preoccupied, and self-serving population of narcissists the world has yet known. (I speak, obviously, of Boomers as a whole; plenty of exceptions could be mentioned.)

Self-indulgence may be the worst way to misuse your giftedness. You can actually be in the sweet spot and thrive as a result, but it's all about you—what you want, what you need, what you think, what works for you.

Money only multiplies the distractions from what matters in life. It can make you indifferent to others, especially those who haven't "made it" yet or never will. And in cases where those people can't be ignored, it makes it easier to just write a check than to get involved. If you're self-centered, you can be very pretty to look at, but you're impossible to relate to, because you don't need anyone. You already have yourself.

However, life has a way of reminding people that making it all about yourself is a bad business. I know a man who told me about getting ready to cash out of a business venture in which he had made a personal fortune. He met three of his buddies for dinner to get their input on life after the payday. They all cheered his success, but then the table fell silent.

Puzzled, he asked them what was wrong. One by one they recounted their own experiences. Each one had similarly thrived in an entrepreneurial venture before selling out. Each one had quickly blown a significant amount of money on a toy—a boat, a plane, a mountain getaway. And each one had gotten divorced.

The man began to poll others in his network. To date he has formally interviewed thirty-nine other men who have sold their companies for a profit. None of them said his life was particularly better for doing that. Almost all of them found that financial independence only made their life more fragile, not less. A number had had affairs and other breaches of character. (He told me, "Bill, who you are before you make the money is who you'll be after you make the money. All the money does is afford you greater opportunities.") Thirty-three were divorced. Many of them turned to diversions like playing golf, purchasing an exotic car, or buying a boat. Most of the ones who did lost interest in their new hobby within eighteen months or less.

My acquaintance summed things up by saying, "Bill, these guys had it all, but every single one of them was in a crisis of meaning."[2]

GOING PASSIVE

At the polar opposite of such superachievers, you can also become like the third manager in the parable of the talents,[3] simply burying your gift instead of investing it. You bury your gift by not using it, for whatever reason. You may be ignorant that you have giftedness (no one who has read this far gets to claim that excuse!), or know about the phenomenon but not know what your gift is. But you can also have a pretty good idea what it is and simply ignore it because some other path appears easier, simpler, or more lucrative.

> Some people treat their giftedness like a jar of spare change forgotten in a drawer.

Occasionally when I work with a corporate client, I run into someone who's on a payroll, but for the life of me I can't figure out why. They show up every day, but they add almost no real value to the organization. One time I asked a guy like that to tell me his story. He said he'd been with the company for years. He didn't feel one way or the other about whether he liked his job. It was just something that paid. He enjoyed going to the racetrack on the weekends, and a few times each year he went gambling in Vegas.

Given the alternatives, I suppose that fellow should be commended for at least paying his way by earning an honest living. But I can't help but feel a tremendous sadness for a life wasted when I run into someone like that. They're just marking time. They're not causing trouble, but then, they're not really doing anything of consequence, either. They treat their giftedness like a jar of spare change forgotten in a drawer.

And some people are just lazy and irresponsible. In the last chapter I described the compounding power of time in turning giftedness to the dark side. In a similar way, sloth is the learned habit of switching off your giftedness and going passive. I'm often asked, which is more important, giftedness or hard work? The answer is, neither is worth anything without the other. Giftedness is squandered on the lazy. Hard work is nothing but toil when you're not gifted to the task. But laziness is a form of negligent disobedience to using your God-given strengths.

WHICH WAY THE MILLENNIALS?

Whatever challenges to making a meaningful life we Boomers have encountered, our children face a vastly different world. Over the past twenty-five years, the rest of the globe has been waking up, growing up, catching up, connecting up, and raising up a new generation of knowledge workers. As a result, if you're a young adult looking for a job today, you're not just competing with your fellow Millennials, you're up against a global workforce that in many cases is equally if not better trained than you are, but less expensive to employ. To make matters worse, you're also up against technologies that grow more powerful by the day, and eliminate more and more jobs that humans have traditionally done.

That scenario is forcing a lot of young Americans and their parents to recalibrate their expectations for the future. There are no more guarantees. There's a lot less margin for experimentation and "finding yourself." Certainly no margin for error.

For those reasons, if you're a Millennial, the two biggest sins that will tempt you are settling and playing it safe. Settling means taking any old job just because you need a job, and then resigning yourself to it by saying, "I guess this is as good as it gets for me. Yeah, I know I have my giftedness and all, but I haven't found anything that fits it. So I'll just hunker down and live my life. Sigh!" Settling means giving up. Punting. I see more and more Millennials just settling, the older they get.

A close cousin to settling is playing it safe—saying no to your giftedness in order to take a job that pays well. Often this gets couched as, "Oh, I know I have my giftedness, and that's great. But I need to make some money first and get financially settled. Then maybe I can come back and pick up this giftedness thing." The advantage of playing it safe is that your parents will almost always affirm you for choosing that option. But what's to say that's not just your own generation's version of, "My will be done"?

WHAT ABOUT YOUR GIFTEDNESS?

I will never tell you what to do with your life. The responsibility for determining that lies solely with you. But I will *always* raise this question: What about your giftedness?

I could not in conscience do otherwise. I know that a great deal in this book flies squarely in the face of prevailing culture. Parts of it no doubt sound preposterous to some. Can this giftedness thing possibly be for real? But I feel like Lucy in *The Lion, the Witch, and The Wardrobe.* She goes into a wardrobe and finds herself in a snowy forest and meets a faun and spends an afternoon having tea with him. When she returns to her siblings, she can't wait to tell them what happened. They don't want to believe her. But she insists that it is so. She can't deny what she knows to be true from her own experience.

> Early on in my life I just gave up and said, "Okay, God. You win."

Neither can I. Having personally listened to thousands of people's stories,[4] I find in each case that there's something there. There's a phenomenon at play. I may not be describing that phenomenon very well or very accurately, and I may be getting the implications of it all wrong. But something is definitely there, something that seems profoundly important and remarkably powerful.

When I then compare those observations with the narrative from the Bible that I hold to, the pieces seem to corroborate in real time with what Scripture asserts about the nature of persons. The only conclusion I can come to is that God has given power to humans. I call that power your giftedness. His intention is that you would use that power hand in hand with Him. True, your giftedness will still "work" if you leave God out. But as I pointed out in the last chapter, using it on your own will almost always turn out badly.

THE KING

So there's no way to avoid it: the question of who owns your life is a problem. And as I just said, I can't tell you how to resolve that problem. I can only tell you how I've tried to resolve it. So while this book has been all about you, from here on out let me talk about me.

Early on in my life I just gave up and said, "Okay, God, You win. Whether I like or not, You made me, which means You own me. My life belongs to You." In short, I kissed the ring of the King and pronounced, "Thy will be done." It's been a wild and crazy ride ever since.

I mean, it can be very difficult to relate to someone you can't see or touch. I've sent up countless prayers over the years. Some of them I know were heard. Many others I've only wondered whether they got through. Coming the other way, I've had a few moments where I knew God was saying something to me very clearly. A lot of other times I haven't heard from Him nearly as often or as clearly as I thought I should. And sometimes there's just silence. Often He says no when I want a yes, and yes when I want a no. A whole lot of the time, He seems to just want me to think on something. And He doesn't always bother to let me in on what's going on, much to my consternation. I know for a fact that saying "Thy will be done" has impaired my reputation and standing in some places, probably cost me a few relationships, and definitely cost me some business.

The worst part about saying "Thy will be done" is that a lot of times I've ended up doing stuff that either I knew at the time was not the King's will, or else realized it was not in retrospect. And to be honest, too much of the time I'm just asleep at the wheel and don't even bother to consider, "What does the King want here?" The result has been many foolish choices and plenty of regrets.

If I sound like I'm complaining about the arrangement between me and God, I'm absolutely not. I'm only saying that trying to honor the ownership agreement between me, a finite and flawed human being, and my Creator is far from easy. Sometimes I do that poorly and sometimes I do it well. Still, the agreement remains in effect.

A lot of my problem, I think, is that I'm a modern-day American, and so I have no real appreciation for what it means to live under a king. In 1776, thirteen colonies in North America did what the first-century Jews were never able to do: they declared themselves free from a tyrant they resented, and they made it stick. As a result, we don't have a monarch in the United States. Every citizen is their own king or queen, and we elect representatives to serve us in governing our land. So when I hear that God is a King who owns me, that's not a metaphor I naturally embrace.

But I gained some insight into the world of kings and queens from which the colonists were emerging when I visited the Palace of Versailles in France. It defines what the palace of an unimaginably wealthy sovereign looks like. And the *piece de résistance* is a long gallery that runs almost the entire length of the western side, called the Hall of Mirrors.

The hall was built in 1690 to impress, and it does, even today. The outer wall is comprised of seventeen floor-to-ceiling windows that look out over the exquisitely landscaped gardens of the palace and the French countryside. Opposite them are seventeen arches of floor-to-ceiling mirrors, which were the state of the art in their day. As the sun set, the hall must have paid dazzling homage to the person who had it built, Louis XIV, *Le Roi-Soleil*—the Sun King.

One use of the hall was to receive royalty, dignitaries, delegations, and ambassadors from all over the world. Imagine the intimidation factor of entering that hall by the southern doors to find a gauntlet of the king's courtiers and other hangers-on turning their heads to see who has arrived. As you traverse that golden corridor, hundreds of eyes study you, scores of murmurs comment on the way you look, how you carry yourself, how you're dressed, and what your business with the king might be.

Raised up on a tall dais at the far north end of the hall is the throne, surrounded by guards, officials, and royal attendants. By the time you come to that pedestal and look up, the entire setting has already told you how things stand: you are the subordinate, you are *granted* an audience with the king, you'll wait for him to speak first, he's in charge, if he wants he can have you removed with a wave of his hand, and if he chooses he can have you shuffled off to prison or carted off to the guillotine. If you're a visitor, he permits your presence. If you're one of his subjects, he owns you and commands your presence.

No one wants to be owned. So even if you have no choice but to subject yourself to the king, you do so because you're forced to, not because you want to. Your allegiance and obedience are secured through fear of his power.

Do you think of God like that—a King who rules through fear? I've encountered a vast number of people who do.

But there's one person I can think of who doesn't feel at all intimidated by the king sitting on his throne in the Hall of Mirrors. This person enters the hall and also walks up the gallery toward the throne. They, too, feel the stares of the onlookers and hear the whispers of the crowd. Finally they arrive at the throne—and keep marching right up the steps, climb up on the king's lap, and say with a smile, "Bonjour, Papa!"

THE FATHER

I may be way off in terms of the way children were viewed in the French court, but you take my point. If the king is also my father, that changes everything. I don't falter in the king's presence like a subject, I walk right up and embrace him as family. I also get certain rights and privileges that nobody else gets. And if you mess with me, well, you mess with the king! There's also the matter of the inheritance.

And so after having said to God so many years ago, "Thy will be done," my experience of Him has been more like God as Father, even though He remains the King.[5] I trust His will for me a whole lot more. Kings like Caesar, or Louis XIV, or George III always rule in light of their own interests. Their subjects matter only as minions in their plans. But God as Father means His plans for me are always going to be for my highest good. Remember what I said in chapter 3? God is infinitely, perfectly good, and He can only treat me according to what is good. I may not always see it that way, and sometimes it's because I can't see it that way, since I don't know all the factors. That's why God is God and I'm me. But even when I don't like His will, I can trust it. I can know that God is for me, not against me.

Having God as my Father also makes me a lot more interested in figuring out what His will is and taking pains to follow it, because I have a vested interest in the outcome. Nowhere has that been more the case than in pursuing a course of life using my giftedness. My giftedness is the most personal expression of God's will for me that I have. It's a built-in way of God saying to me, "Bill, here's what I want you to do with your life." Knowing that has answered a thousand questions and no doubt helped me avoid a million problems.

Yes, I still have to think, make choices, and ask for guidance. The King's will is not a script. But like an improv actor who's been given a role and a scenario, I've got a direction. I've got a foundation to work with. I know when it's my turn to contribute my lines—as well as when it's not.

THE VOICE

What I'm talking about here—indeed, what this whole book is about—is the issue of *calling*. We've managed to complicate this thing of calling so much that no one can agree what it means anymore. Even I—who as you can see has a gift for taking things that are very simple and complicating them all out of proportion—find the whole discussion of calling to be bewildering.

But I'm not sure it's really that hard to grasp. A call is just that—a voice that is calling out.[6] Not just speaking but summoning, eliciting, perhaps commanding. In this case, we're talking about the voice of God.

The Voice calls out and there's a world. Years later The Voice calls out and there's a person—me. The Voice calls to me and says, "Follow Me." At some point I say, "Okay. Thy will be done." From then on The Voice begins a pattern of calling out, "Bill, here's what I want you to do for now."

A lot of what The Voice calls me to do is embrace whatever opportunities I'm given and use my giftedness to make a contribution to the world and earn a living. Depending on many factors, some within my control and most outside of it, I may become financially successful in following that call. Or I might not.

But sometimes The Voice calls, "Don't worry so much about the money part on this activity. Just do it because it matters. I've got purposes in view that go way beyond what you can know about." And so I do something that may not pay much or at all but is significant nonetheless. My role as a parent fits into this category. So does the work I'm doing through my church for the benefit of some children in our community.

And then sometimes The Voice calls, "Bill, I actually don't want you to use your gift right now. I want you to set it aside and do this thing just because it needs doing, and if you don't, no one else will." I can think of toilets that needed to be cleaned, garbage that needed to be taken out, adult supervision that needed to be present, rides that needed to be given, and many other mundane tasks I've done along those lines. No one is particularly gifted to those activities. But like Jesus taking off His robe to wash the disciples' feet, sometimes The Voice asks me to just serve.

And every once in a while The Voice calls, "Bill, I have something for you that's going to prove costly. You're going to pay a price to do it." And I find myself giving away some time or money or personal convenience or whatever, something I'd really prefer to keep for myself. But the need is urgent, and The Voice has called me to just give myself away.

I've even heard The Voice say, "Bill, on this one you're going to take a real hit. I'm not even going to ask you to give something away; I'm going to take something away. Something you care about a lot. And it's going to hurt. I want you to trust Me anyway. I'll walk with you through it all. But this is what has to happen." And so again, I've ended up sacrificing. And The Voice was right. What happened was not simply inconvenient, it was downright wounding. I didn't like it one bit. But when the King says it's time to go into battle, even if you're His son—*especially* if you're His son—you don't balk or grow cowardly. You say your prayers, and then, "Yes, m'Lord."

Everything turns on the question of who owns your life. I don't know anyone who says "my will be done," living the way I've just described. Instead, their life always seems to end up being all about them. But I've known plenty of people who have said "Thy will be done," living exactly as I've described. I have yet to find one of us who regrets having said it.

> To know Him is to find yourself.

One day The Voice will call to me, "Come on home." And if Jesus is to be believed, once I get there The Voice will say, "Bill, well done!" Unless it says, "Who are you? I never knew you."[7]

What a strange question that The Voice may ask: "Who are you?" Why, that's the same question you've been asking your whole life! "Who am I?" Imagine asking that question forever, but never finding the answer. If that should happen, The Voice says it will only be because "I never knew you." I can't think of a more compelling statement that your very identity is inextricably bound to the One who made you in the first place. To know Him is to find yourself. And knowing yourself only makes sense if you know Him.

What about the "well done"? Well, that's His reply to my saying, "Thy will be done." That's shorthand for, "Yes, Bill, thank you. My will *was* done!" And what is His will? That I would be me, just as He made me. That I would do my "good works," just as He gave me. That He would see Himself in me, and in doing so, He would revel in infinite delight.

DISCOVERING YOUR GIFTEDNESS: A STEP-BY-STEP GUIDE

There's only one you! Which means you "do life" in a thoroughly unique way. In the following exercise, I'll help you discover a very consistent pattern to the way you function. You live out that pattern again and again throughout your life. That pattern describes your giftedness in action.

Note: In the interest of saving space, this section of the book is just an overview of the Discovering Your Giftedness assessment on the Giftedness Center's website (www.thegiftednesscenter.com). If you have Internet access, I strongly recommend that you use the online version of this process, as it offers a lot more information and guidance in completing it, and you'll get a much better result.

Before You Begin
You find your pattern by doing two things:

(1) *Telling Stories*
First I'll show you how to tell several stories from your life, in your own words.

(2) *Looking for a Pattern*

Next I'll help you analyze your stories to find a wonderful and consistent pattern in the way you were designed you to function.

How much time will it take to complete this exercise? Well, you can spend as much or as little time on it as you'd like. Obviously, you'll get more out of it if you give it the time it deserves. But on average, it should take about six to eight hours to complete. You may prefer to spread it out over two or three days.

Of course, some people end up deciding that it's just easier to have a professional take them through a formal assessment of their giftedness, just as they would pay someone to change the oil in their car, or do their taxes, or decorate their home. If that's the case for you, I'd be more than happy to arrange for that. You can contact me through the information in the back of the book, or through the website.

But I think most people can get pretty far on their own, and for a lot less money, by completing the exercise below with a partner.

TELLING STORIES

The best way to discover your giftedness is to see it in action from your own life history.

Your life is a story in which you've done many things and many things have happened to you. You can probably recall all sorts of events, milestones, achievements, experiences, successes, failures, and so on.

Out of those many life stories, certain stories are about an activity you enjoyed doing, felt a sense of satisfaction from doing, or gained energy from doing. We call stories like that your *Giftedness Stories*.

Giftedness Stories

There are two criteria for a Giftedness Story:

(a) it must be about an *activity*, something you did, something that required effort and action on your part; and

(b) it must be about something you *enjoyed* doing or took *satisfaction* from doing.

Here are several examples of Giftedness Stories that people might remember:

- Age 5—I memorized a poem and recited it to my kindergarten class.
- Age 16—I made a birthday cake for my younger brother.
- Age 23—I volunteered for a Big Brother program and worked with an eight-year-old boy. I specifically remember one time when we visited the zoo and he told me he wanted to work with animals when he grew up.
- Age 28—Developed a database for our marketing team.
- Age 40—Set up our family's budget and finances on my computer. I use it to manage our expenses and stay within budget.
- Age 58—Taught my granddaughter to sew.

Giftedness Stories can come from any period of your life—childhood, teen years, adult years up to the present.

Giftedness Stories can also come from any area of your life—personal life, school, work, home, sports, leisure, hobbies, volunteer involvements—wherever you *enjoyed* the activity. Satisfaction is the key!

Your Turn

Use the sample Giftedness Stories given above to come up with your own list of Giftedness Stories below.

Try to come up with at least twelve to fifteen stories (although feel free to come up with as many as you want).

Remember: Giftedness Stories are about activities that were satisfying to *you*. You're going to tell these stories to another person. So list activities that you'll feel comfortable talking about.

AGE At time of activity (optional)	GIFTEDNESS STORY Brief one- or two-sentence description

Recruiting a Partner

Now that you've come up with your list of Giftedness Stories, you'll need to tell those stories to someone else. Who should that person be?

- Someone you feel comfortable with.
- Someone you trust.
- Someone who knows how to listen.
- Someone who can refrain from commenting too much.
- Someone who can remain neutral and just let you tell your stories.

The truth is, almost anyone will do, as long as they can agree to let you tell your stories. That person might be a friend, coworker, neighbor, minister, youth worker, roommate, college professor, or someone else with whom you have enough of a relationship to feel comfortable. (However, I advise against recruiting a member of your immediate family or someone else with whom you have a close emotional or psychological connection.)

You might ask: "Why do I need to tell my stories to anyone? Why can't I just write them out?" You're welcome to write them out (there's more information about how to do that on the website). But having been involved with this process for three decades, I must tell you that there is a powerful and undeniable benefit from telling your Giftedness Stories to another person. I can't fully explain why that is so. I just know it is so. Besides, doing it with a partner is a lot more fun!

So if you really want to make this work, find a partner.

If you'd like a script to help you know what to say in recruiting your partner, you can find one on our website.

Your partner doesn't have to read this book to help you (although it wouldn't hurt). However, it will definitely help if they review this section of the book, along with chapter 5, "The Truth Hidden in Plain Sight," so they understand the logic of this process and what their role is.

How This Process Works

You need to tell eight Giftedness Stories to your partner. To do that, go back in your mind's eye and relive the activity. Tell your partner what they would have seen you doing if they had been there, watching everything as it happened. Describe in as much detail as possible *what* you did and *how* you did it.

Never mind *why* you did it! We just want to see you in action.

When you're finished telling your partner what happened, then describe what was *satisfying* to you about doing that activity. What was it that you enjoyed about it?

As you can see, this exercise may be different than anything you've done before. But it's as simple and straightforward as it sounds. Don't try to overthink it!

An Optional First Step: Write Out Your Stories

Some people find it helpful to write out their stories before they tell them to their partner. Writing helps them remember and record details that they might forget to include if they just start telling their stories "cold."

This prework is optional, because not everyone likes to write. But if you are so inclined and have the time, it will certainly benefit the process.

Instructions for Telling Your Stories

(1) Find a partner, as described above.

(2) Set a time and place to tell your stories. Choose a spot where you won't be interrupted or distracted. Set aside or disable any communication devices.

(3) Plan on about an hour to an hour-and-a-half to tell your stories.

(4) If you want, make a recording while you tell your stories. That way, you'll be able to go back later and check the details of what you actually said.

(5) Follow this format in telling each story:

First, set the story up by establishing the context and describing how you got involved in the activity.

Next, walk your way through the story, describing in as much detail as possible the main steps and key actions you took. Help your partner "see" you doing this.

Finally, describe what was satisfying about the activity. What did you most enjoy about doing it? Don't just say, "I liked it." See if you can put a description to that satisfaction.

(6) As you tell your stories, your partner should write down some of the key words you use, especially:

Action words (verbs). For example: planned, taught, evaluated, read, built, arranged, etc.

The things or people you worked on, with, or through. For example: dog, team, machine, guitar, idea.

Notice the blank Giftedness Story form (p. 214). You'll find a link to that form on the website. Print out eight of those pages for your partner to use in recording the details of each story.

Also notice the sample Giftedness Story page filled in on p. 215.

(7) Tell your partner a total of eight Giftedness Stories. If you wrote out your stories as described above, use those. If not, just pick eight, preferably from different periods of your life. You might even consider letting your partner choose which stories you tell.

(8) Count on taking between ten and fifteen minutes to tell each story. If you're finishing your stories in five minutes or less, you're probably not giving enough detail. On the other hand, if you're spending twenty minutes per story, you may be going into irrelevant details.

(9) When you've finished telling your stories, take a break. You've earned it! You may want to schedule another time to meet with your partner to look for your motivational pattern. Just do whatever feels most comfortable to you.

Some Advice for Your Partner

As the partner, your job is to help the storyteller tell their stories using the format described here. The fact is, most people find this exercise a bit daunting, and perhaps even intimidating. They've never done anything like this before, and they worry that they're not going to do it "right." You can be a support by reassuring them and helping them follow the instructions given.

You can find more suggestions and information on your role in this process at the online version of this exercise.

LOOKING FOR YOUR PATTERN

You've told eight Giftedness Stories to your partner. Now it's time to look for a unique pattern of behavior and motivation that your stories reveal.

What Do I Mean by a "Pattern"?

A *pattern* is something that repeats itself on a fairly consistent basis. For example, suppose someone tells eight Giftedness Stories, and in five of those stories the person describes working directly with animals. That's a pattern—an element or theme that repeats throughout a story.

To find these patterns in your Giftedness Stories, you need to analyze your stories. This involves two steps:

First, you must sort out the details of each story.

Then, you must examine the details to see which of them recur throughout the stories.

Sorting Out the Details

Set a time for you and your partner to get together again. Your partner's involvement will be invaluable, because they bring an extra set of eyes to this part of the exercise. They also bring their memory, along with some helpful perspective.

GIFTEDNESS STORY FORM

Storyteller _____

Your Name _____

STORY:

KEY WORDS AND DETAILS

SATISFACTION: What was the satisfaction in doing this activity?

GIFTEDNESS STORY FORM

Storyteller __Jay__

Your Name __Andrew__

STORY: Refurbished a park to earn Eagle Scout badge.

KEY WORDS AND DETAILS

my responsibility—think through details, logistics

organize everything—make a list—call city—information —requirements

explain project to other scouts—recruit their help

draw layout—make a plan—where things would go

find dirt—arrange for dump truck

round up tools—call to Lowe's—meet with manager— fill out form—pick up donated materials—stone—plants

be the leader—coordinate meeting time—get there early— outside—weather

gave assignments—see how it all was going—team

sign off on completion—quality

thank everybody

award

SATISFACTION: What was the satisfaction in doing this activity?

completing the project and handling the responsibility

On p. 219 is a form entitled Giftedness Story Summary. You'll find a link on the website to that form. Print out eight copies to use in capturing the details from each of your Giftedness Stories.

For each story do the following:

(1) In the top box labeled *Story*, write a brief title or description of your story.

(2) The next box is labeled *Abilities.* Look carefully at your story. What abilities did you use in this story? Action words (verbs) are usually the clues to the abilities you used.

Using the notes that your partner wrote down on your Giftedness Story Form, along with your own written summary (if you wrote one), work with your partner to identify the abilities you used in your story and list them in the box labeled *Abilities*.

(3) The next box is labeled *Subject Matter*. Look carefully at your story. What things or people were you working with in this story?

Whenever you use an ability, you use it on, with, or through something. For example, in the illustration above, the storyteller was frequently found working with animals. Likewise, an accountant would work with numbers. A day-care worker works with children. A girl studying for a history exam might be working with information and facts. An actor works with an audience.

Work with your partner to identify the various subject matters you used in your story and list them in the box labeled *Subject Matter*.

(4) The next box is labeled *Circumstances*. Look carefully at your story. What circumstances or conditions were you operating under in this story?

Circumstances are about the environment you were in. Was there stress and pressure? Or were things calm and quiet? Were there a lot of people involved, or just you? Were you working toward a goal? Were things flexible and unstructured? Was there a deadline? Was there an audience watching you? Were you being recognized, or were you more behind-the-scenes? Were you outdoors, or perhaps in a lab?

In short, where did your story take place? What were the conditions that were affecting how you did your activity?

Work with your partner to identify the circumstances you were in, in your story and list them in the box labeled *Circumstances*.

(5)   The next box is labeled *Role*. Look carefully at your story. How did you relate to the other people in this story?

When you're using your giftedness, you tend to relate to others in a certain way. We call that a "role." In your stories, you may have been a participant on a team. Or maybe the leader of the team. Or perhaps you weren't the leader, but you played a key role on the team. Maybe in the story you organized everything. Maybe you functioned more like a teacher or coach or mentor. Of course, it's possible there were no other people in your story, or even if there were, you functioned on your own, as an individualist. There are many possibilities for what role you played in your story.

Work with your partner to describe what role you played in your story and write that in the box labeled *Role*.

(6)   The last box is labeled *Satisfaction*. Look carefully at your story. What was the satisfaction you described in this story?

The first place to look in answering that question is the box on the Giftedness Story Form labeled Satisfaction. What did your partner write down when you described what was satisfying about the activity in this story?

Another way to identify the satisfaction is to step back and look at the story as a whole to notice what it's about and what you were trying to accomplish.

Work with your partner to try and describe the satisfaction you gained from the activities in your story and write that description in the box labeled *Satisfaction*.

(7) When you've completed the Giftedness Story Summary for your first story, it should resemble the sample Giftedness Story Summary on p. 220.

(8) Fill out a Giftedness Story Summary for each of your seven other Giftedness Stories.

Note: You can find examples for what I mean by Abilities, Subject Matter, Circumstances, Roles, and Satisfaction on our website.

Making the Connections

Now that you've identified the relevant details from your eight Giftedness Stories, you need to look for a pattern by determining which ones repeat and recur. On p. 222 is a formed entitled Giftedness Patterns. It looks similar to the Giftedness Story Summary form, but it's designed for you to collect your observations from all of your stories onto a single page. You'll find a link to that form on the website. You only need to print out one copy of the Giftedness Patterns form.

Here are the steps for filling out that form:

(1) Lay out the eight Giftedness Story Summaries that you and your partner completed. Look at the abilities listed in the boxes for *Abilities* on the eight summaries. What do you see repeating? List them in the box labeled *Abilities* on your Giftedness Patterns form.

(2) Now move to the items listed in the boxes for *Subject Matter* on your eight summaries. As you did with Abilities, compare the eight summaries to identify what subject matter you regularly work with. List those elements in the box so labeled on your Giftedness Patterns form.

(3) Next look at the items listed in the boxes for *Circumstances* on your summaries. Compare the summaries to identify what circumstances are common among your stories. List those in the box so labeled on your Giftedness Patterns form.

GIFTEDNESS STORY SUMMARY   Storyteller _____

STORY:

ABILITIES—What abilities did you use in this story?

SUBJECT MATTER—What things or people were you working with in this story?

CIRCUMSTANCES—What were the circumstances or conditions you were in, in this story?

ROLE—How did you relate to the other people in this story?

SATISFACTION—What was the satisfaction you described in this story?

GIFTEDNESS STORY SUMMARY   Storyteller __Jay__

STORY: Refurbished a park to earn Eagle Scout badge.

ABILITIES—What abilities did you use in this story?

think through	call
organize	meet with
make list	fill out
call	pick up
explain	be the leader
recruit	coordinate
draw	get there
make plan	give assignments
find	see how it was going
arrange	sign off on completion
round up	thank

SUBJECT MATTER—What things or people were you working with in this story?

details, logistics	dump truck	materials
list	tools	stone
information	Lowe's	plants
other scouts	manager	
dirt	form	

CIRCUMSTANCES—What were the circumstances or conditions you were in, in this story?

responsibility	team
requirements	completion
project	quality
outside	award
weather	

ROLE—How did you relate to the other people in this story?

Leader

SATISFACTION—What was the satisfaction you described in this story?

completing the project—handling responsibility

(4) Move on to the items listed in the boxes for *Roles* on your summaries. Identify what role is common in your stories (there may be more than one). Write that role in the appropriate box on your patterns form.

(5) Now it's time to evaluate the satisfaction that keeps repeating in your stories. Look first in the boxes for *Satisfaction* in your summaries. Do you notice a consistent theme?

In addition, step back and look at the big picture of each of your stories. What are they about? What are you trying to do in these stories? Is there a common theme that describes the sort of activity you come back to again and again?

Discuss with your partner the common theme (or themes) of satisfaction that your stories show. See if you can boil it down to a brief description. Then write that phrase into the box labeled *Satisfaction* on your Giftedness Patterns form.

Note: As you look for patterns, realize that you may not have used the exact same words in each story, but it's obvious that the same or a similar element is involved.

For example, in one story you might have said, "I read the instructions," while in another story you said, "I turned to the owner's manual." Those are different words, but the same kind of ability is involved—namely, "reading."

If you've provided enough detail in telling your stories, you should see certain elements repeating in at least three or four stories, if not more. If you don't see any elements repeating more than once or twice, you need to go back and provide more details about how you did the activities in your stories, and/or what was so satisfying. Don't speak in generalities. Get specific. Describe exactly what you did and what was satisfying, even if it seems obvious to you.

(6) When you've completed the Giftedness Patterns form, it should resemble the sample form on p. 224.

GIFTEDNESS PATTERNS

Storyteller _____

ABILITIES—These are the abilities you commonly use in your stories.

SUBJECT MATTER—These are the things or people you commonly work with in your stories.

CIRCUMSTANCES—These are the circumstances or conditions that are common in your stories.

ROLE—This is how you commonly relate to other people in your stories.

SATISFACTION—This is the satisfaction you commonly experience in your stories.

LOOKING AT THE BIG PICTURE

Congratulations! Once you've completed your Giftedness Patterns form, you have a description of the consistent pattern you use in your life. It's a picture of your giftedness—of you in action:

- You know the Abilities you consistently and comfortably turn to in accomplishing your ends.
- You know the Subject Matter that you most enjoy working with and through.
- You know the Circumstances that are ideal for you.
- You know the Role that you prefer to play relative to others.
- And you know the consistent Satisfaction that drives your behavior, the motivational outcome that you most enjoy and seek.

That's fantastic! Did you know these things about yourself? If so, had you realized how prevalent your pattern was throughout your life? If not, what new discoveries have you made by telling your Giftedness Stories and analyzing them?

Some Questions to Ask

(1) What does your pattern tell you about:
- how you learn?
- how you make decisions?
- how you relate to groups and teams?
- how you fare if you're on your own?
- who you need around you to be effective?
- how long you're liable to stay motivated on an activity?
- how you communicate?
- the kinds of work you should and shouldn't do?

(2) Now that you have the "big picture" of how you function, how does that account for the successes and disappointments you've experienced in life?

(3) How might your pattern affect other people around you—your family, friends, coworkers, customers, neighbors?

GIFTEDNESS PATTERNS   Storyteller __Jay__

ABILITIES—These are the abilities you commonly use in your stories.

make arrangements   ask questions, inquire
plan   convince, persuade
decide   be the leader
listen   coordinate
explain   recruit
set goals   assign
draw   check up on, monitor
figure, calculate, estimate promote, talk it up
organize

SUBJECT MATTER—These are the things or people you commonly work with in your stories.

details   key individuals   humor
tools, gear   stories   systems
information   money, budgets
groups   spaces, places
logistics, arrangements materials

CIRCUMSTANCES—These are the circumstances or conditions that are common in your stories.

outdoors, nature   team, group   challenges
responsibility   finished product   awards
project   quality, excellence deadlines
time to prepare   requirements
entrepreneurial   goals, objectives

ROLE—This is how you commonly relate to other people in your stories.

project coordinator

SATISFACTION—This is the satisfaction you commonly experience in your stories.

getting a finished product—taking responsibility

(4) In what situations would someone with your pattern be especially valued? Where would you likely be devalued or misunderstood?

Follow-Up Suggestions

(1) Show your pattern to those closest to you—your spouse and family, your parents, your boss, a coworker, a close friend, etc. What is their reaction? Do they confirm and validate your findings?

(2) Based on your pattern, write a description of your ideal job.

- What would you be working with?
- What natural abilities would you be using on a day-to-day basis?
- What would be the circumstances of the job?
- What would be your role?
- What would be the ideal way for your boss to manage you? Or do you even require a boss?
- What would be the satisfaction or "payoff" that you regularly receive from your work?

Now how does that ideal scenario compare to the situation you are currently in?

(3) Assuming your current situation is not a good fit for your pattern, what might be some ways to improve that fit? (See chapter 8, "Giftedness and Your Work," for more on the issue of job-fit.)

How might you express your pattern outside of work, perhaps through a hobby, volunteer activity, or activity that you do at home?

(4) Keep your Giftedness Patterns page handy as you read through the rest of the book.

NOTES

Chapter One: A Pattern in Your Life

1. Alice Schroeder, *The Snowball: Warren Buffett and the Business of Life* (New York: Bantam Books, 2008), 94.

2. Ibid., 117–18.

Chapter Two: What Is This Thing Called Your "Giftedness"?

1. Jim Collins, *Good to Great* (New York: Harper Collins, 2001), 210.

2. Richard John Rhodes, *James Audubon: The Making of an American* (New York: Alfred A. Knopf, 2004), 4.

3. Alice Ford, *Audubon By Himself* (Garden City, NY: Natural History Press, 1969), 4.

4. Rhodes, 5.

5. Ibid., 143.

6. William Wordsworth, "My Heart Leaps Up," based on John Milton's lines from *Paradise Regained*: "The childhood shows the man / As morning shows the day."

7. Peter F. Drucker, *The Practice of Management* (New York: HarperCollins, 1954), 151.

8. Daniel Levitin, quoted in Malcolm Gladwell, *Outliers* (New York: Little, Brown and Company, 2008), 40.

9. Clare Sheridan, *Nuda Veritas*, as cited in Virginia Cowles, *Winston Churchill: The Era and the Man* (New York: Grosset & Dunlap, 1953), 32.

10. Learn more at http://landfillharmonicmovie.wordpress.com, where you can find a link to a video about this project, which I strongly encourage you to view. For a similar insight into the presence of giftedness among people with very little power, see the video "Xu Bing and the Phoenix," which tells the story of Chinese artist Xu Bing discovering remarkable creativity among migrant workers building the World Financial Center in Beijing. Go to www.youtube.com/watch?v=hu4sD4c6yXA&feature=youtu.be.

228 • THE PERSON CALLED YOU

11. M. Scott Peck, *The Road Less Traveled* (New York: Touchstone, 1988), 13.

12. Rosaria Champagne Butterfield, *The Secret Thoughts of an Unlikely Convert: An English Professor's Journey into Christian Faith* (Pittsburgh: Crown & Covenant Publications, 2012), 135.

13. Genesis 11:1–9.

Chapter Three: The Good Truth about You

1. The quote has an interesting backstory. According to the late photographer Nat Finkelstein, it came about while he was photographing Warhol as part of a book project in 1966. Onlookers were doing what onlookers often do, trying to get themselves into the shots. According to Finkelstein, Warhol blurted out that everyone wants to be famous. Finkelstein shot back, "Yeah, for about fifteen minutes, Andy." Warhol later used the line in the program for an exhibition of his work in Stockholm. See Jeff Guinn and Douglas Perry, *The Sixteenth Minute: Life in the Aftermath of Fame* (New York: Jeremy P. Tarcher/Penguin, 2005), 4, 364–65.

2. Psalm 139:13–16 NIV.

3. The Hebrew word translated "dust" simply means the ground or earth. The context of the passage shows that the ground was still barren and had not yet been broken up by plants, and that a mist watered it, implying it must have been wet and somewhat compact—not unlike clay. The Jewish historian Josephus (c. 37–100 AD) wrote that the first man "was called Adam, which in the Hebrew tongue signifies one that is red, because he was formed out of red earth, compounded together" (*The Antiquities of the Jews*, I, 1:2). In Job, Job's friend Elihu begins his remarks by reminding Job that he, too, is a created man, saying, "The Spirit of God has made me, / And the breath of the Almighty gives me life . . . Behold, I belong to God like you; / I too have been formed out of the clay" (Job 33:4, 6).

4. The theme of God designing people from the womb surfaces again and again in both the Old and New Testaments. If you want a case study in giftedness showing up early and recurring throughout a person's life, read the story of Joseph, recounted in the last third of Genesis. You'll find that from an early age, Joseph was put in charge of his father's sheep (37:2). A few years later, after his brothers sell him into slavery, an Egyptian military officer named Potiphar puts him in charge of his household (39:4). Framed by Potiphar's wife, he ends up in prison, where the warden puts him in charge of the other prisoners (39:22). When the pharaoh has a troubling dream and none of his wise men can interpret it, his cupbearer remembers that Joseph interpreted one of his dreams when he was in prison. So Joseph is fetched and he interprets the pharaoh's dream. In appreciation, Pharaoh puts Joseph in charge as prime minister over all of Egypt (41:41). As a result, Joseph eventually has authority over his own brothers—exactly as he had foretold when he was a youth. Clearly, the motivational pattern of Joseph's life, beginning from the womb, was to be in charge, to be in control, to exercise authority over others. Indeed, so strong is Joseph's giftedness for exercising authority that as he lays dying in Genesis 50, we find him using his last breaths to give orders to his children and their descendants as to where his remains should eventually be buried. Even from the grave, Joseph wants to be "in charge"!

Other examples where the Bible talks about God designing people from the womb include Job (10:8–12; 31:15), Moses (Exodus 4:11), Samson (Judges 13:5), Jeremiah (1:5), Paul (Galatians 1:15), the nation of Israel (Isaiah 49:1, 5), and people in general (Psalm 33:13–15). Countless other supporting passages and themes could be mentioned. All of it underscores the fact that God designing people from the womb is a basic teaching in Scripture.

5. Genesis 1:26–27 NIV.

6. Colin Welland, "Chariots of Fire" (script) (London: Enigma Productions Ltd., 1980), C29, p. 82-A.

7. Interestingly, that's as true of so-called "saints" as it is of miserable sinners. As Paul struggles with the "good news"/"bad news" of his own heart in Romans 7, he finally cries out, "Wretched man that I am! Who will set me free from the body of this death?" (v. 24). Later he wrote Timothy that "Christ Jesus came into the world to save sinners, among whom I am foremost of all" (1 Timothy 1:15). That's no different from the tax collector who could not even raise his eyes to heaven as he cried out, "God, be merciful to me, the sinner!" (Luke 18:13). There is a long parade of people in history who have recognized the utter poverty of their soul and cried out to Christ for mercy—not just when they first came to faith, but especially after decades in the faith.

8. With God we can never ask, "What did He know and when did He know it?" He knows everything, and He has always known it and always will.

9. There's a lot of other Scripture to support the contention that we are *always* on God's mind. Psalm 139 itself opens with a rhapsody on God's constant awareness of David: "You know when I sit down and when I rise up; / You understand my thought from afar. / You scrutinize my path and my lying down, / And are intimately acquainted with all my ways. / Even before there is a word on my tongue, / Behold, O Lord, You know it all" (vv. 2-4). Jesus, in the Sermon on the Mount, points out, "your Father knows what you need before you ask Him" (Matthew 6:7). Later He encouraged His disciples that they could trust the Father because "not one [sparrow] will fall to the ground apart from your Father. But the very hairs of your head are all numbered. So do not fear; you are more valuable than many sparrows" (Matthew 10:29-30). In Romans, Paul writes that "the Spirit Himself intercedes for us with groanings too deep for words" (v. 26). In the same chapter he adds that Jesus is also right beside His Father interceding for us (v. 34; see also 1 John 2:1). The Trinity ceaselessly pays attention to us!

10. See William Shakespeare, "As You Like It," Act II, Scene V, monologue by Jacques: "All the world's a stage, / And all the men and women merely players."

11. Interestingly, Psalm 8, also attributed to David, actually suggests that very thing: "What is man that You take thought of him, / And the son of man that You care for him? / Yet You have made him a little lower than God, / And You crown him with glory and majesty!" (vv. 4-5). The word for "God" here (*Elohim*) has given translators fits for as long as people have been translating this passage. That's because the word means "god," and in the Old Testament refers to THE God with few exceptions. It's the same word used in Genesis 1:1: "In the beginning God (*Elohim*) created the heavens and the earth."

12. Psalm 14:1-3. Note that this is also a psalm attributed to David, who wrote Psalm 139. Paul cites Psalm 14 in Romans 3:10-12 to make the point that all humanity is fallen and broken and locked in sin.

13. Romans 3:23.

14. Ephesians 2:1.

15. Psalm 51:5 NIV.

16. See Philippians 2:5-8 and 2 Corinthians 5:21.

17. Psalm 139:1-6.

18. Psalm 139:7-12.

Chapter Four: Your Purpose, Your Power

1. C. S. Lewis, *The Lion, the Witch, and the Wardrobe* (New York: Harper Trophy, 1950), 117–18.

2. Ephesians 2:10.

3. The Greek word is *poeima*, the word from which we derive the English words "poem" and "poetry" (until fairly recently, poets were not said to "compose" a poem, but to "make" a poem). However, Paul is not thinking of poetry but of a more tangible form of artisanship.

4. Ephesians 2:10 has traditionally been understood as a purpose statement for the universal church. "We" is interpreted collectively, as in "we believers, we the church" have been created in Christ Jesus for good works—those works generally understood as the spreading of the gospel and its associated acts of mercy, compassion, justice, and standing up for God's truth. However, just as we individually were "dead in [our] trespasses and sins" (vv. 1–3), so we individually have been "made... alive together with Christ" (vv. 4–7). And just as we individually are "saved by grace" (vv. 8–9), so we individually are Christ's "workmanship, created in Christ Jesus for good works" (v. 10).

5. C. S. Lewis, *A Preface to Paradise Lost* (Oxford, England: Oxford University Press, 1961), 1.

6. Genesis 1:28 THE MESSAGE.

7. I see nothing in Genesis 1:28 that precludes humans from accessing and using resources beyond planet Earth—the Moon, other planets, asteroids, conceivably other bodies in other solar systems and/or galaxies.

8. Having said that, it's interesting to read what God says when He sees the people of the ancient world building the Tower of Babel: "If as one people speaking the same language they have begun to do this, then nothing they plan to do will be impossible for them" (Genesis 11:6). Apparently God is quite aware of what humans collectively are capable of doing.

9. Work is described as "the gift of God" in Ecclesiastes 3:13 and 5:19.

10. Many people buy my premise that God has outfitted each of us with natural talents and abilities to accomplish the everyday work of the world. But what about "spiritual gifts"? How does what I'm saying about giftedness relate to them? That question deserves a book unto itself. But the short answer is: I *am* talking about spiritual gifts. Giftedness and spiritual gifts turn out to be the same thing. However, let me be quick to add, most of what is taught today on the matter of spiritual gifts is received tradition that really needs to be reevaluated in light of what Scripture actually says. Some of what is taught has little or no basis in the Bible. And of course the whole area of the "gifts of the Spirit" (which turn out to be different from what most people mean by "spiritual gifts") is a matter of considerable debate.

11. I'm using the word "work" broadly here. Homemakers (whether women or men, married or unmarried) don't get paid for their work, but it's work nonetheless. Likewise, someone with a trust fund might be independently wealthy and occupy their time playing the guitar or visiting Machu Picchu. Nevertheless, for purposes of this paragraph, those pursuits qualify as their "work." Work involves how one devotes the time and energy of their life.

12. The truth is, God has a *great* deal to say about your work. I could steer you toward countless excellent resources on that, but here are five that I have personal experience with: the Theology of Work Project (www.theologyofwork.org); LeTourneau University's Center for Faith and Work (www.centerforfaithandwork.com); the Center for Faith and Work at Redeemer Presbyterian Church in New York City (www.faithandwork.org); the High Calling (www.thehighcalling.org); and Princeton Faith and Work Initiative (www. princeton.edu/faithandwork).

13. International Labour Organization, "Global Employment Trends 2013" (Geneva, Switzerland: International Labour Organization, 2013); available at *http://www.ilo.org/wcmsp5/ groups/public/---dgreports/---dcomm/---publ/documents/publication/wcms_202326.pdf.*

14. Author(s) unnamed, "Toward the end of poverty" (*The Economist*, June 1, 2013); available at *http://www.economist.com/news/leaders/21578665-nearly-1-billion-people-have-been-taken-out-extreme-poverty-20-years-world-should-aim.*

15. Like all of us, the founding fathers and framers of the US Constitution were people of their times. The options they envisioned extended primarily to white males, but not to females or black slaves. They left it to later generations to expand their insight into "unalienable Rights" to all US citizens.

16. In the last twenty-five years, the world has seen significant freedoms brought about in countries like Poland, former East Germany, Russia, China, Vietnam, and many others. Sure enough, the economies of those countries have exploded—not without turmoil and challenge, to be sure, but bristling with options unheard of in previous generations. I in no way endorse unbridled capitalism, but I do believe that wherever people are free to exercise their God-given giftedness, the world becomes remarkably more "fruitful," just as Genesis 1 predicts.

Chapter Five: The Truth Hidden in Plain Sight

1. The Myers & Briggs Foundation, www.myersbriggs.org/my-mbti-personality-type/my-mbti-results/how-frequent-is-my-type.asp.

2. "Flow" is the state of being fully energized and engaged in an activity. I regard it as the physiochemical expression, and indeed evidence of giftedness. See Mihály Csíkszentmihályi, *Flow: The Psychology of Optimal Experience* (New York: Harper & Row, 1990).

Chapter Six: Warning: Identifying Your Giftedness Is Not Enough

1. Luisa Kroll and Kerry A. Dolan, eds., "Oprah Winfrey: The Forbes 400: The Richest People in America," *Forbes*, as of September 2013. www.forbes.com/profile/oprah-winfrey.

2. Federal Bank of New York, "Regional Economic Press Briefing," June 27, 2013, 17. www.newyorkfed.org/newsevents/mediaadvisory/2013/Presentations_06272013.pdf.

3. Proverbs 22:7.

4. For more on this way of thinking about life, see Patricia Ryan Madson, *Improv Wisdom: Don't Prepare, Just Show Up* (New York: Bell Tower, 2005).

5. You can read more about our family's story and how God showed up for us in our darkest hour in my book, *The Light That Never Dies: A Story of Hope in the Shadows of Grief* (Chicago: Northfield Publishing, 2005).

6. Mark Twain quoted in Victor Donyo, ed., *Mark Twain: Selected Writings of an American Skeptic* (Amherst, New York: Prometheus Books, 1983).

7. I estimate that roughly 60–65 percent of people naturally think in terms of goals. The other 30–35 percent think in terms of concepts, relationships, learning opportunities, adventures, stories, and other categories that are not at all goal-oriented.

8. See B. Joseph Pine II and James H. Gilmore, *The Experience Economy, Updated Edition* (Cambridge, Mass.: Harvard Business Review Press, 2011).

9. Available at www.bls.gov/ooh.

10. Blogger Sherry Surratt credits this wisdom to Carey Nieuwhof, lead pastor at Connexus Church in Ontario, Canada. She did not say whether it is original with him. Her blog can be found at http://sherrysurratt.wordpress.com.

Chapter Seven: Giftedness and Your Work

1. Susan Sorenson, "How to Tackle U.S. Employees' Stagnating Engagement," *Gallup Business Journal*, June 11, 2013. http://businessjournal.gallup.com/content/162953/tackle-employees-stagnating-engagement.aspx.

2. No one exactly knows who came up with the two-box diagram. I first saw it in 1985 when Ralph Mattson used it to explain job-fit to me. At the time, Ralph was working with Art Miller Jr. at People Management, Inc. (PMI, now SIMA International, Inc.). After I became a part of People Management in the 1990s, I saw numerous uses of the diagram by various other practitioners. I once asked Art where it originated. He credited a client from the 1960s and '70s named Jim Meiklejohn at Connecticut General. Over the years I've seen a handful of variations of the diagram, the main one being two circles overlapping rather than two boxes.

3. "The mass of men lead lives of quiet desperation." Henry David Thoreau, *Walden*.

4. Kim Murphy, "Bill Gates: How to be super-rich, or save the world trying," *Los Angeles Times*, October 28, 2011. http://latimesblogs.latimes.com/nationnow/2011/10/bill-gates-university-of-washington.html#comments.

5. Steve Jobs, Commencement Address at Stanford University, 2005.

6. See Eric Brynjolfsson and Andrew McAfee, *Race against the Machine: How the Digital Revolution Is Accelerating Innovation, Driving Productivity, and Irreversibly Transforming Employment and the Economy* (ebook published by Digital Frontier Press, October 2011), available at http://raceagainstthemachine.com.

7. For example, Helen Keller, Anne Frank, Aleksandr Solzhenitsyn, Eric Liddell, Nien Chang, Viktor Frankl, Elie Wiesel, Dith Pran, and Oscar Pistorius, to name just a few.

8. NPR Books report on Jim Wooten's book *We Are All the Same: A Story of a Boy's Courage and a Mother's Love* (New York: Penguin Books, 2005), entitled "One Boy's Heroism in the Face of AIDS"; available at http://www.npr.org/templates/story/story.php?storyId=4195336.

9. I say "we" because my sister Bev Godby works with more mothers than I do. In truth, if a book on giftedness and mothering ever gets written, Bev is the one who should write it.

10. Oliver Wendell Holmes, "The Voiceless."

Chapter Eight: Giftedness and Your Relationships

1. 1 Samuel 16:7 NIV.

2. Psalm 33:15 says that God "forms the hearts of all" (NIV).

3. 1 Peter 3:7.

4. Proverbs 22:6.

Chapter Nine: Giftedness and Your Dark Side

1. I don't want to be too dogmatic about describing David's giftedness. The text portrays him in a certain light. Whether that presentation perfectly matches the actual man is impossible to say. David's story can be found in the books of 1 and 2 Samuel and 1 Chronicles. A great deal of information can also be gleaned from the Psalms and numerous other references to David in Scripture.

2. 1 Chronicles 28:3.

Chapter Ten: Giftedness and Your Calling

1. Matthew 22:15–22 THE MESSAGE.

2. You can read more about Rogers Kirven's story at www.maninthemirror.org/weekly-briefing/503-the-rogers-kirven-story.

3. Matthew 25:14–20.

4. I'm by no means the only person to have done that, nor did the techniques for doing that originate with me. Bernard Haldane began looking at people's successes in the 1940s. Art Miller Jr. apprenticed under him in the late 1950s and early 60s, then started his own firm called People Management, Inc. (now SIMA International, Inc.). Hundreds of thousands of people have gone through the SIMA process that PMI developed. Ralph Mattson offers a similar process called DOMA. In addition to those practitioners and their colleagues, the whole field of psychometrics attests to the fact that people are unique. And in recent years, a psychology of positive human functioning, or positive psychology, has gained wide interest through the work and writings of Martin Seligman at the University of Pennsylvania, and Mihaly Csikszentmihalyi, formerly of the University of Chicago and now at Claremont Graduate University.

5. I get to take such liberties with God only because I'm invited to do so. That's one of the huge contributions of the New Testament. Jesus refers to God as His Father 165 times in the Gospels, and encourages me as His follower to do the same. The formal prayer that He gave begins with, "Our Father." Later Paul wrote that those who have the Spirit of Christ instinctively call out to God, using the term, "Abba," meaning Father—or closer to the term's actual usage in Paul's time, Poppa.

6. The New Testament verb for calling (*kaleo*) means just that: to call, call loudly, invite, or call by name. Illustrations of calling are abundant throughout the Bible, but the concept is especially developed in the New Testament, where "calling" begins to get used in what might be called a technical sense. To my reading, that's where things have gotten murky. Christ calls His first followers, and God in Christ has been calling people to Himself ever since. The apostles frequently use the terms "call" and "calling" throughout the Epistles. Theologians have tried to parse all those different uses to the point where it's no longer clear whether there is one "general" call, or a general call followed by some special call, and perhaps other special callings.

7. See Matthew 7:23 and 25:14–30.

ACKNOWLEDGMENTS

I'm often asked how long it takes me to write a book. In this case, the answer is about fifty-nine years. Indeed, a lifetime of people have contributed to what I've written here. So many that if I named them all, I'd end up with another book almost as long as this one. I have a very good memory for people who have proven helpful to me, even ones who didn't know they were helping. But I'm sure I'm going to leave out someone who deserves mention as I thank those who have supported me in this project and express gratitude for those who have shaped my thinking.

First, I've had the benefit of a long line of mentors—honestly, too many to mention. One of them whom I never got to meet was Bernard Haldane. To my knowledge he was the first person in our time to inquire into giftedness in an intentional way. His protégé Art Miller Jr. became a valued friend and colleague, and Art's insights into personhood have been foundational in my work. His former colleague Ralph Mattson was the genius who made the connection for me between giftedness and what is called a theology of persons.

Art founded a company that today is known as SIMA International, Inc., of which I am a member. Over the years I've gained an ocean of insight from interacting with my SII colleagues. I particularly must call out Dick Staub, Bill Banis, John Paris, Art Miller III, Kim Miller, Steve Darter, Nick and Judy Isbister, Rick Wellock, Rob Stevenson, Tommy Thomas, Ed Poff, Ron Evans, Marlys Hanson, Mark Stevenson, Suz Grimes, Josh Miller, and the amazing Don Kiehl, to whom I owe so much.

I have Bob Buford to thank for introducing me to Ralph Mattson, an encounter that changed the course of my life. It's a great example of how one can never be too careful about putting people together! Bob may live the most intentional life I've ever seen, and he is impacting a strategic population of his peers through his Halftime Institute.

As this book shows, a lifelong theme for me has been the intersection between faith and work. I have countless people to thank for letting me sit at their feet on that issue, especially Pete Hammond, Doug Sherman, Ray Bakke, Dennis Bakke, Bob Shank, and all my associates with the Theology of Work Project—Haddon Robinson, Tom Phillips, Andy Mills, Al Erisman, Randy Kilgore, Cheryl Kilgore, Gordon Preece, Will Messenger, Kathryn Leary Alsdorf, Cara Beed, Bill Heatley, L.T. Jeyachandran, Clint LeBruyns, Alistair Mackenzie, Alice Matthews, Sean McDonough, Dave Williamson, and John Stahl-Wert.

So many friends have aided and abetted me in my odyssey: Bob and Jerrie Moffett, Bob and Elaine Dibbs, John and Linda Sorensen, Bill and Sally Murdoch, Tom and Kate Newcomb, Jesse and Carolyn James, Len and Carol Crawford, Tracy and Carol Wood, Larry and Susan Lincoln, Bill Wellons, David and Lilian Barger, Don Johnson, Dave Naugle, Wayne Smith, Reggie McNeal, Steve Roese, John Maisel, Kurt Nelson, Wayne Nance, Keet Lewis, Andy and Gail Seidel, Fred Smith Jr., Susan Knape, Robbie Briggs, and Nathan Pratt. Cal and Sue Boroughs are not only friends but family. I'm forced to leave so many other names out.

Three people I owe my life and sanity to are Alex Vasquez, Jim Coté, and Jonathan Dick.

Bill Peel and I have been driving on the spike of giftedness together for twenty-five years or more (with his wife, Kathy, cheering us on). A more recent coconspirator is George Coleman, who knew all about giftedness at the street level before I even arrived at the party.

My Wednesday morning group has been an invaluable source of

strength, support, and stability: Ben Albritton, Russ Miller, Clanton Harrison, and Brad Smith.

Many people were gracious enough to keep me in their prayers as I wrote. Four that I haven't named elsewhere here are Scott Hanson, Dave Steane, Jed Robyn, and the treasure named Lyn Baker.

For reasons I cannot explain but certainly do not question, Moody Publishers keeps rolling the dice on me by publishing my work. I have years of gratitude built up for Greg Thornton and his team. On this project I get to thank Duane Sherman for raising my sights on what my theme needed to be, Betsey Newenhuyse for her editorial prudence and discernment, and all of the specialists who contributed their giftedness for design, production, marketing, distribution, and other publishing particulars. Many of you I've never met, but your work has made mine possible.

Thank you, Carol Turpin, for the gracious hospitality of your lake house, your consistent prayers, and your affirming smile.

Family looms large in whatever I've been able to accomplish. I've mentioned my dad, Howard, several times. I know his impress on me is more than I even realize. I guess what I most appreciate about Dad, and what ultimately benefited me the most, was that he remained true to his giftedness despite financial adversities, temptations to sell out, personal limitations and struggles, and the seductions of success. I think part of his genius as a teacher was that he could intuitively recognize the giftedness of a student and play his part in unleashing it. So I feel like I'm carrying on his legacy.

My Mom has been a mother. A mother is the only person in the world who somehow always has you on her mind no matter what else she may be doing. Mom has always believed in me, most especially in this crazy thing I do related to giftedness.

My brother Bob schooled me in giftedness and helped me lay a foundation for much of the work that the Giftedness Center does today. No doubt many ideas presented here originated with his profound insight into personhood, and especially its implications for teams and organizations.

And then there's my sister and compatriot, Bev Godby. This book could easily have been a coauthorship, and perhaps should have been, because every page and every idea reflects something that Bev and I have discussed a thousand times. Bev has been my Samwise Gamgee, loyally and tenaciously beside me every step of the way—even when I have been unworthy of her. If you want to know the deeper truths of the purposes for why we are here and what really matters in life, spend some time with Bev. But be prepared! She will look into your heart, and she won't shrink back from telling you what lies in the deeps.

And I would be remiss not to also thank Dale Goby, Bev's husband. As a clinical psychologist, he does a masterful job of reminding me that people are very complex, and there's so much we don't know, and at the same time, so much we're finding out. But I value so much the way he encourages Bev and me to continue to hone our craft and get our message out.

I can't say anything about giftedness without acknowledging the contribution of my first wife, Nancy, who died in 2000. Nancy's maternal instincts "got" giftedness long before I was even literate on the subject.

I have Nancy to thank for Brittany, Kristin, and Amy. You don't get to choose your children, just as your children don't get to choose you as their parent. But that's why these three women are such gifts to me, because I could never have chosen so well. It's one thing to talk about giftedness to others, and to help my clients embrace it. But to get a front row seat watching my daughters emerge into the world in all their glory has been nothing short of breathtaking. I thank God for them every day.

My wife, Lynn, has been my biggest supporter. Born to participate, I can only imagine what it must feel like for Lynn when I isolate myself in order to pull together my thoughts and words. I practically have to go dysfunctional to get it all done. Long-suffering Lynn has graciously and gracefully endured that craziness. I owe her a great debt of gratitude, and probably a long vacation to boot.

Finally there is the One whom this book is about. All along I've said it's about you, and so it is. But as I pointed out in the final chapter, if it's about you, it's about God, too. Whatever truth this book contains, whatever good seeds it plants, whatever impact it makes, whatever significance it ultimately has are all derived from Him. I'm only a tool in His hand. I just pray that my gift has served Him well.

Soli Deo gloria

ABOUT BILL HENDRICKS

Bill Hendricks is president of The Giftedness Center, a Dallas-based consulting firm specializing in organizational effectiveness and individual career guidance. Bill is the author or coauthor of twenty-two published books. He has also written for numerous publications, and his thoughts can be found at his blog, BillHendricks.net. He holds an undergraduate degree in English from Harvard University, a master of science in mass communications from Boston University, and a master of arts in biblical studies from Dallas Theological Seminary. He is a board member for Pine Cove Christian Camps and sits on the steering committee for the Theology of Work Project. He is married to Lynn, and is also the father of three grown daughters.

The Giftedness Center™
www.thegiftednesscenter.com

BILLHendrICKS.neT

YOU COULD BE
A GIFTEDNESS COACH

If you want a make a real and lasting difference in someone's life, I can show you how to help people wake up to their giftedness and then walk with them as they find and start following their purpose. I call that role a Giftedness Coach.

Giftedness Coaches are invaluable, because only a tiny fraction of people are able to grow and make progress solely on their own. Most everyone needs a coach. A coach is someone who will listen, encourage, make suggestions, provide feedback, lend perspective, provide accountability, and otherwise support a person's efforts to realize their good intentions. In short, a coach is someone who cares enough to walk alongside someone in their journey.

You may already be working in a certain occupation because it allows you to help people that way. I'm thinking of teachers, professors, school administrators, deans of students, athletic coaches, counselors, therapists, social workers, pastors, youth workers, staff members at camps and conference centers, staff of youth programs like Big Brothers and Big Sisters or Boy Scouts and Girl Scouts, community center directors, corporate trainers, personal coaches, spiritual directors, chaplains, and similar vocations.

However, almost anyone can get in on the action. To find out more, go to the link for Giftedness Coaches on The Giftedness Center's website:

http://www.thegiftednesscenter.com